My First Six-Months Leadership Trial: Lived Experience and Personal Statement – Learning Derived

Table of Contents

Career Summary

After I was accredited as an R.N. in Washington State, I worked in several institutions including the Largest Psychiatric Hospital located in Washington State and worked in several Nursing Homes. I did my field work residency at one of the Franciscans Hospital in Washington State. I became a Nursing supervisor in July 2018. Also, I earned a Master of Nursing at the University of Washington in June 2018.

My master's degree fieldwork endeavors provided me with skills to integrate theories and knowledge into practice, as evidenced by many executive summaries and recommendations that I have written, data aggregations and analyses, making several PDSA (Plan-Do-Study-Act) cycles for continues improvements as well as PICO (Patient-Intervention-Comparison-Outcome) model utilization, an action plan with the use of logic model and creation of

SMART   (Specific-Measurable-Achievable-Relevant-

Timely) objectives.

Author's Background

I started my career as a volunteer at the largest Psychiatric Hospital located in the Western part of Washington State last October 2012. My volunteer job helped me understand the lifestyle here in America, where I immigrated, away from my immediate family in the Philippines. My volunteer job has indeed been a rewarding job; it is priceless, as it helped me to grasp who I am today. I am thankful for the support and guidance the University of Washington during my school year there and proud to be an Alumni of University of Washington, America. Above all, thank you to the Almighty!

My Leadership Style Analysis and Self Reflection

I was born and raised in the Philippines. I have 11 siblings: three brothers and eight sisters, and two of them were adopted. I am the oldest girl in the family. Being the oldest girl was a big responsibility. I had to help my mom a lot in cooking, cleaning, and caring for my younger brothers and sisters. I grew up in a rural area where I needed to walk four miles to school every day. Many times, I had to walk on rice patties with bare feet on rainy days. Despite these inconveniences and challenges, I appreciate the opportunity of being able to go to school.

I attended my high school in an urban area while I was working in an orphanage home as an assistant chef. At that time, I met my late husband, who was a veteran of the US army, and we were married for 16 years. After my husband and I moved to the U.S., I was accredited as an R.N. in Washington State and worked in several institutions, including the largest Psychiatric Hospital in Washington

State, and several nursing homes. I have been in different positions: charge nurse, nursing supervisor, clinical risk management and admissions coordinator Nurse. I care about my job and patients. Patients are the reasons why I was pursuing my master's program in leader in healthcare delivery at the University of Washington, which I graduated from in June 2018. I wanted to be able to offer my competencies in leadership in healthcare delivery at the largest Psychiatric Hospital in Washington State. I plan to improve patient care, provide guidance for the workforce, and improve the nursing work environment.

When I was 17 years old, I started serving the orphanage home currently known as Happy Home. I was serving the missionaries and church people. I stayed working with Happy Home for six years. During those years, while I was working with Happy Home, I was cooking and serving food for missionaries, acting as a chef assistant, as well as doing housekeeping jobs. I learned to take responsibilities and work with gratitude, knowing that I am serving people from different countries such as England, Norway, Sweden, and America. Due to this experience, I learned about different cultures as I got to observe different languages and styles, especially eating habits and foods. I learned that a leader does not have to be rigid to be successful in leading. Similar to one influential leader and writer, John Maxwell "understands the golden rule as an effective leading principle of integrity in every situation" (Mesner-Andolsek &Sumi, 2017, p. 29). Integrity reflects a healthy organization as it reflects how the workers behave and express their opinions and values and how the leader creates a kind of work environment climate that is free of intimidation and bullying (Edmonson & Bolick, 2017). Both ethical and moral standards are necessary for the success and existence of an organization and the success of a leader (Mesner-Andolsek &Sumi, 2017).

Challenges

As a nurse supervisor and a leader who is young and growing, one of my challenges is the nature of my workplace; it is dynamic and diverse. It always has newly hired staff coming in for training. All newly hired nurses have different backgrounds, experiences, and learning styles. Conflict is inevitable because of the power struggle between newly hired and senior staff. As a nurse supervisor, I support that - respect, integrity, and fairness for all members of my team. This way, I am role modeling a culture of a great team, free of intimidation and abusive behaviors.

Strengths

My strength is **humility and compassion** to serve not just patients but also all staff members, as well as being responsible for my organization's policies, rules, and regulations. Supporting and motivating staff members through a shared vision and mission – my flatform in my leadership is to "improve nursing care environment by providing guidance and support to nursing staff and therefore helps improve quality of patient care." Helping people to do things they weren't sure they could do by giving encouragement and praise. Giving positive feedback.

Adaptable – Working with psychiatric patients and multicultural staff – any situation can arise unexpectedly, and as a leader, I need to be able to handle things… be able to adjust…. and modify my approach to a certain or uncertain, unpredictable situation. Adapt how to best serve the community.

Detail oriented - to be able to make a smart goal, we need detail, and we analyze the data, and we get results…detail will help us to plan and identify problems that may arise in the future and prepare solutions and implement solutions quickly and deliver high quality of work.

Optimistic and Loyal – it is necessary to be able to work my best even in the most difficult situations. For example, when I was a nursing supervisor on the ward, I covered 7 -

wards on weekends and the next day, I got down deployed, and I still smiled – why? Because I am thankful/grateful for being able to serve the community – it is gratitude! – that keeps us healthy, happy, and productive. Loyalty is being able to communicate without fear of getting in trouble. "I got you," "you have my back; I have your back" – loyalty. I will back you up. I will be there, and you are, and you will – that's loyalty. And it is postering a positive climate. We don't have to be rigid to be successful leaders like the influential leader and writer John Maxwell. He believes in the Golden Rule as the driving principle of integrity – do unto others what you would like others do unto you.

Weaknesses

Introverted versus extroverted personality type: I am 50 percent introvert and 50 percent extrovert. So, if you see me being quiet today and the next day, I am talkative – that's how I am.

Humility: I must know that if I am too humble, people might perceive or interpret that to me as a weakness because I am already small. I must compensate and have a voice. We need to understand and sometimes admit that there are things that we cannot control and things that we cannot do (from the author's journal). We need to delegate as appropriate. We need to let go of our insecurity and ask for help. Also, being able to adapt or adjust, depending on the situation. Working with psychiatric patients and multicultural staff, there are always uncertainties and unpredictable circumstances that can arise at any moment. It is like abstract; you don't know what comes up – it is unpredictable. We need to adapt to changes as they come and go while achieving the goal. Adapt how to best serve the team in certain situations. Adapt even during very limited resources (from the author's journal). Also, being detail oriented and knowing details will help to plan and identify problems that may arise in the future. Detail allows the leaders to prepare solutions to potential problems and implement these solutions quickly and effectively. Being thorough will help to improve a leader's decision- making abilities to identify and correct errors and be organized (from the author's journal). Loyalty is very important in the sense you are not punitive. During difficult situations, this loyalty pays off; staff will show up for each other and support each other. Loyalty means looking past mistakes and errors for the sake of the relationship. Loyalty is important because it establishes an emotional commitment and strengthens relationships, particularly when life gets difficult. Loyalty is inspiring, listening, motivating and bringing out the best in employees - poster positive climate. Relationships with loyalty are stronger because both people can be themselves and share what they're experiencing without fear that another person will abandon them (from the author's journal). Loyalty stands for commitment and dedication to your values and mission statement, being true to yourself.

Humility – humility in leadership is the key to building authentic leadership connections. Be valuable sometimes or be real with others. We can't be perfect all the time. Pride is concerned with who is right. Humility is a concern with what is right. Learn to accept that you might be wrong. Being willing to convene the pain of not always being right. This way, I can reassess myself.

Self- reflections and analysis, practices to help to continuously improve and grow. "It is not about who is right; it is about what is right" (taken from the author's journal). Accept compliments and constructive criticism. I will listen to you, and I will humble myself – this is wisdom. Learn how to appreciate other's success and growth and celebrate it for them. Do not be a selfish and arrogant leader. Instead of feeling jealous, step forward and strive to improve self. Do not be resentful of other's progress.

Ambitious: like to look good. Ambitious people will strive towards difficult goals. I work hard and study hard; I want to be successful. I want a higher level of myself and my company. Multifaceted. I pushed myself to succeed. After all, why are we striving if we do not have ambitions? Ambitions can be bad if you are setting up unrealistic goals.

My Leadership Philosophy

My leadership philosophy is that leaders are also managers; therefore, they need good management skills, and they have followers and subordinates. Although, when they lead, they have to give up authoritarian control because it is a voluntary activity to follow the leader. Leaders influence others through their charismatic abilities. They empower and motivate people towards meeting goals and vision. Leaders focus on people, influence people to do things and work besides people. I believe that there is no such perfect leadership style. A combination of all leadership styles might be best, depending on where you are working. I believe that quality leadership is supportive of staff and maintains and develops a work environment full of healthy employees or individuals physically, emotionally or mentally, and financially.

The autocratic leadership style should only be used in situations of crisis; Laissez-faire observes followers working from a distance and only intervenes when needed, while democratic leadership is supportive of group interaction and decision-making. Every nurse is a manager because he/she plans, organizes, motivates and controls to effect of quality patient care (Clancy, 2008; Foltin & Keller 2012; Giltinane, 2013; Kalisch, Weaver, & Salas, 2009; Maccoby, M., Norman, C. L., Norman, C. J., Margolies, R. 2013; Murphy, 2005).

In my experience as a leader, I go to work on scheduled time; I dress appropriately- neat and tidy. I take responsibility by being there at my scheduled time of work and meetings and being sincere in everything I do-smile and greet people. I initiate help if others need help. I was a leader when I mentored newly hired nurses at my workplace because I worked beside them, and they followed me, learned, and became good at the job like me. I have worked as a night shift charge nurse- full time and an on-call charge nurse, in the nursing home. Now, I am currently working as a nursing supervisor/charge nurse-full time in a psychiatric facility.

During emergencies, I am an authoritarian because I want things done the right way and to save lives. I do not just talk; "my adrenaline rush makes me do as I talk in a life-threatening situation". For example, I had 3 types of patients in 1 shift: patient A- Difficulty of Breathing (DOD)/Shortness of Breath (SOB), patient B- complaint of a fainting spell and a week-old heart valve surgery, patient C- complaint of severe pain with crying, grimacing, guarding and moaning behaviors. I had 2 nursing assistants, 22 patients and 1 admission coming up from the hospital that day, and at the same time, I had to make sure that these 22 patients' medications would be given on time as scheduled and their wounds to be treated properly in my shift. I had to prioritize, of course; I commanded one assistant to get the vital signs. I am running to get the oxygen since our assistants are not allowed to give oxygen. I made independent nursing action by giving 2L/M of Oxygen to the patient having SOB/DOB right away and observed his condition. While I was intervening with the patient, I shouted or signaled, asking for vital signs for patient B. Patient B- BP was very low, so I instructed my assistant to put the patient in a T-position and at the same time, I grabbed a pain medication to the patient who was in severe pain and focus assessment done, of course. Anyway, the shift went alright; all patients were safe. I then reviewed/studied their medications and dosing and then contacted the MD for medication adjustments, informed them about patients' situations and documented all nursing/physician's interventions accordingly. While during ordinary hours, I give space to my subordinates, I do not micromanage my colleagues, and I remind them to go to take a break because I do not want them to get exhausted and burned out. I showed them my care and made sure too that our jobs were done properly.

I wanted to share my experience with my manager, who brought coffee for me one time; as she walked towards me, she had two Starbucks coffees in her hands, approaching me with a very nice smile. I was so happy and grateful to her that I didn't consider refusing the coffee or telling her that I do not drink coffee. As she handed me the coffee, I smiled and said, "Thank you," and then accepted the coffee. After about an hour or two, my supervisor found out that I do not drink coffee (my co-nurse told her), and I was able to explain to her the truth—It's the thought that counts.

At my current work, there are days that I focus more on tasks due to an overload of paperwork to do and tasks to assign to subordinates. As a charge nurse, I have to do a quick decision to assign subordinates to a certain task such as 1:1 therapeutic monitoring, suicidal risk monitoring, seclusion, restraint, meal monitoring for critical diabetic patients, risk for dehydration, and unable to feed self. Each of those tasks has an underlying paperwork to process for the whole shift. I am doing incidence reports for falls, assaults, altercations, wounds, bruises and whatever situation arises during that shift, such as a patient needing a transfer to emergency or just in-the-ward treatment for intravenous fluids and catheterization. I deal with the treatment team with patients' previous and present conditions, medication updates, laboratory works, treatment planning, and plan addendums. I am dealing with patient leaves, appointments, and family visits. The hardest thing I have ever experienced was when I realized that most of my subordinates that day were floats or on calls, especially if they had never been to the ward because they did not know the patient, and I had to orient them, too, each time. These are the times when I say to myself, I need a cup of hot chocolate drink, or else I am going to cry.

I have also experience working where with some of my subordinates that been working in the same ward for more than a decade; it is really hard being a charge nurse when it seems you cannot tell them what to do and act like they know everything and not open to new ideas— "what do you know, you are only new here." It was complicated when I just started, but I had confidence that I could manage them through hard work and communication. But I said what I had to say anyway until it got stuck in my mind, and I understood each other's expectations, and we became a good team. My experience with my team: One time, I was asking for some help. I yelled, "Staff! Staff! Staff!" - This means I needed more staff because the patient was combative and uncontrollable, and I could not handle it just by myself (I was new, and I was not charging that day). I was assigned to the floor as a floor RN doing direct patient care. No one had helped me then, until a few minutes later, the charge nurse assigned that day finally came out and helped, and nobody else. It could have been too late, and I'm knocked out. This is an example of lacking teamwork in my team.

Truly, I believe that a team player is a good quality nurse. Passing the ball to others for the whole team to win or be successful, and if that team member only gets the credit, it's ok; there's no competition. We are a team. My strength as a leader is that I have a big heart. At work, every beat of my heart is utilized for my patients, my colleagues and the organization I am working with. At the end of the day, I am happy; I am content because I know I did my best. I also have a touch of brain- enough to manage difficult people at my workplace and enough to manage difficult situations.

Conflict is unavoidable in a group or team. (I can say that there is always something after another conflict situation.) Each of the members is unique, especially since we are all from different upbringings, and different cultures and traditions. During conflict time, I empathize with both members and analyze things without reacting and judging both because maybe, and usually, it is just a burnout moment and nothing big or personal. I had an experience with my two female CNAs (Certified Nursing Assistant) who argued very seriously. One CNA yelled at another, and I heard it so loud in the patient's hallway. I came out and went to the hallway without a word. The one who yelled walked to the nurse station while the other continued whatever she was doing, "changing the patient's diaper." I did not follow the one who yelled because she was still agitated, so I gave her space. I looked at the one being yelled at and came closer to her. She looked at me for a second, and I touched her shoulder and as soon as I touched her shoulder, she then cried like a baby. I do not know what I really did as a leader (charge nurse at that moment), but after that, they gradually became friends. The situation was never brought to the management. The conflict was resolved.

One needs to know how to work in a group. According to Kalisch, Weaver, and Salas, (2009), Nursing depends on teams to carry out its mission and objectives. Nurses stay in jobs where teamwork is effective. Effective teams are more productive and less stressed nurses, which produce higher quality care, fewer errors and more patient satisfaction.

Each day I go to work, I always tell myself that I am a nurse and that I am not going to work just to take care of my patients; I am also a nurse to my colleagues, and I care for them too. Giltinane (2013) the ability to identify own feelings and emotions can also identify followers' emotions accurately. Giltinane et al. (2013) nursing leaders motivate, inspires, empowers or influences others by doing direct clinical care to ensure that proper nursing care is provided to the patients. Foltin, and Keller (2012) Emotional Intelligence leader uses empathy and social skills, recognize and use what works best for each individual in establishing norms to maintain the momentum of change implementation phase and prevent staffs from slipping back into old routines

References

Clancy, T. R. (2008). Managing organizational complexity: Control: What we can learn from complex systems science. Journal of Nursing Administration, 38 (6), 272-274.

Giltinane, C. L. (2013). Leadership styles and theories. Nursing Standard (royal College of Nursing (Great Britain): 1987), 27, 41, 12-18.

Foltin, A., & Keller, R. (2012). Leading change with emotional intelligence. Nursing Management, 43, 11, 20-5.

Kalisch, B. J., Weaver, S. J., & Salas, E. (2009). What does nursing teamwork look like? A qualitative study. Journal of Nursing Care Quality, 24, 4.

Maccoby, M., Norman, C. L., Norman, C. J., Margolies, R. (2013). Transforming health care. Hoboken: Wiley.

Murphy, L. (2005). Transformational leadership: a cascading chain reaction. Journal of Nursing Management, 13, 2, 128-136.

Culminating Paper

My career goal was to lead clinical systems improvement at the largest Psychiatric Hospital in Western Washington, United States.

This is a culminating paper that will review coursework from both T EDUC 502 and T NURS 512. T EDUC 502 is about Learning about Learning, and T NURS 512 is about Evaluation of Academic and Clinical Performance in Nursing and Healthcare. These two courses serve my professional needs as they align well with my curriculum goals to be an effective leader in healthcare delivery. I enrolled and completed T EDUC 502, Learning about Learning, in the Autumn quarter of 2017. T EDUC 502 is about behaviorist, cognitive, constructivist, and sociocultural theories, which would be useful for a nursing leader to understand the educational processes in healthcare. I took T NURS 512, Evaluation of Academic and Clinical Performance in Nursing and Healthcare, in the Spring of

2018. This course equipped me with knowledge in evaluating academic and clinical performance in nursing and healthcare. It involved activities such as analyzing a variety of assessment procedures for use in academic nursing education and nursing professional development, summarizing social and legal issues impacting the evaluation of educational outcome achievement, analyzing methods used to evaluate learning and program outcomes, and applying program planning and evaluation principles including cost-benefit analysis and clinical outcome measures to evaluate educational program effectiveness.

These two courses helped me to prepare myself to deal with the constantly changing nursing and healthcare environment because I became competent in learning theories, teaching strategies or methods, and rationalized curriculum development. Learning theories provide guidance in dealing with each student's learning as they provides the foundation for curricular content and pedagogical innovations (Keating & Zuccarini, 2015). Learning theories provide reminders to healthcare leaders about the importance of complex educational content, challenging cognitive tasks, self-efficacy, professional role modeling, information organization, and regard for students (Keating & Zuccarini, 2015).

TEDUC 502 Course Specifics

In addition to getting knowledge of different learning theories, I came to understand how to analyze and critique theories in T EDUC 502. For example, I applied social learning theory principles in my role as a charge nurse in a Psychological Rehabilitation Program (PRP) ward. On the other hand, the entire workplace is very dynamic and diverse; it always has newly hired nurses and other nursing staff coming in for training. This class is a great help in a way that I am able to understand different learning theories and teaching and learning strategies to mentor and precept the newly hired nurses. It helped me to understand the psychological and socio-psychological learning process in order to teach and counsel individuals, families, and communities. Through T EDUC 502, I gained deeper knowledge, skills, and a better attitude in dealing with how people act or learn in a certain way, with consideration of their culture, behavior, and cognitive abilities through the analysis and application of learning theories.

T EDUC 502 Course Description

T EDUC 502 "Learning about Learning" is about examining behaviorist, cognitive, constructivist, and sociocultural theories of learning. Specifically, it is about analyzing and critiquing each theory as it applies to classroom teaching.

Alignment with Leadership Option and MN Program goals

This course T EDUC 502, "Learning about learning," is important for me as a leader in healthcare delivery because it helped me to explore different learning theories. This course helped me effectively analyze and critique theories in order to guide in teaching and counselling individuals, families, and communities in the context of psychological and socio-psychological areas of the learning process. I learned how to prepare and organize a seminar-type presentation and how to lead a small discussion. I have also learned how to compare and contrast as well as critique and evaluate the effectiveness of learning models in relation to classroom experiences. I have expanded my understanding of the psychological and socio-psychological contexts within the educational processes and enhanced my pedagogical knowledge and skills. The mission of the course is "To prepare ethical and reflective educators who transform learning, contribute to the community, exemplify professionalism, and promote diversity." After completing the T EDUC 502, I will be able to:

- Evaluate the adequacy of underlying knowledge from nursing science, related fields, and professional foundations as it informs nursing practice.

- Competently assess and manage health-related issues with a defined population or care system and evaluate the effectiveness of these nursing practices.

- Demonstrate competence in the development of inquiry relevant to practice, education, or administration.

- Gain competencies in clinical outcomes management.

When I took T EDUC 502 in the Autumn of 2017, I learned different perspectives on education. I gained more confidence in my learning style and how various forms of teaching have affected me. I realized that constructivist principles are what I have been utilizing in studying in nursing school and doing fieldwork.

Behavioral learning theory is what I have been utilizing at work every day for these past few years. My team is using behavioral theory to solve some problems occurring in the care of our psychiatric clients. My team provides a social learning program, such as token economy to our clients who have shown only limited benefit from regular programs. Token economy structure focuses on individual prompts, response – contingent consequences, social and material reinforcement, and individual associative learning. Results are the reduction or elimination of aggressive behaviors, including changes in frequency, intensity, or timing of distressing mannerisms. Followed by the development of improved self-care, social skills and communication skills, as well as improved interest in motivational to engage in vocational, leisure and housekeeping tasks. This is important for psychiatric clients to prepare for their full recovery from psychiatric illness and be discharged in the community successfully. Another important concept of behavioral learning theory is modeling the behavior. My team demonstrates the behavior we are trying to teach to psychiatric clients. When the psychiatric clients show appropriate behaviors, we give immediate rewards, such as attention, praises for each achievement of tasks, and tokens. This way, we are gradually shaping healthy and socially appropriate behaviors. My clients can use tokens to buy stuff at the token store, which includes candies, sodas, chips, nutritious bars, and accessories that are safe for them to use.

Now, in my own classes, I can see which theories and principles my professors are applying, for example, watching video clips, lectures, PowerPoint presentations, writing, making graphics/symbols on the board, and small group discussions on different topics, which are constructivist ideas. We also watched a video clip that explained behavioral theory and played a game on blood transfusion. After learning, I am feeling more confident in accepting responsibilities as a master's prepared RN. In this course, I learned that teaching and learning have to be flexible, as each student is unique and has different experiences or situations in life. It is important to consider all learning theories, concepts, and theorist perspectives as well. I also believe that there are more factors to be considered in educational approaches, such as the learner's socioeconomic status, preferences, environmental conditions, as well as physical, emotional or psychological well-being.

Taking this course allows me to have the competence in managing clinical outcomes such as:

- Evaluate the adequacy of underlying knowledge from nursing science, related fields, and professional foundations as it informs nursing practice.

- Competently assess and manage health-related issues with a defined population or care system and evaluate the effectiveness of these nursing practices.

- Demonstrate competence in the development of inquiry relevant to practice, education, or administration.

- Gain competencies in clinical outcomes management.

As a nurse leader, I will use theory-based approaches in program planning for health management and disease prevention. I will use theories to establish goals and objectives, as well as monitoring and reinforcement. I will use the theories to guide myself to solve problems. Once I obtain my master's degree, I want to help improve patient care, provide guidance for the workforce and improve the nursing work environment at Largest Psychiatric Hospital.

T NURS 512 Course Specifics

The other course option – TNURS 512, includes activities such as assessing and evaluating academic and clinical performance in nursing and healthcare. The most important learning experience for me in T NURS 512 was creating a test blueprint for nursing students. I also applied various assessment techniques in developing exam questions and appraised different evaluation tools and criteria. Learning about formative and summative evaluation approaches makes me understand how to apply either or both approaches in assessing performance in nursing practice. I learned the importance of simulation which can be used for assessing competencies. These will help me to prepare leadership skills in staff development, curriculum development and continuing education, and most importantly will help me for the evaluation of clinical performance at my current workplace at Largest Psychiatric Hospital.

TNURS 512 Course Description

T NURS 512, "Evaluation of Academic and Clinical Performance in Nursing and Healthcare". Examines concepts of assessment and evaluates learning and performance in academic and healthcare settings. This course also teaches us how to analyze a range of assessment strategies in formative and summative evaluation and how to apply program planning and evaluation principles to educational interventions in the academic and healthcare delivery setting.

Description of how this course will serve my professional needs

T NURS 512 serves my professional goals through preparing my leadership skills on staff development, curriculum development and continuing education, and evaluation of clinical performance. For example, health education strategies can be used to facilitate continuing education in all settings, such as in schools, hospitals, and communities.

Alignment with Leadership Option and MN Program goals

Completing T NURS 512 allows me to meet the below MN program goals:

- Develop skills related to healthcare management, evaluation, and ethics of health care systems and organizations.

- Gain competencies in clinical outcomes management.

- Evaluate policies that relate to healthcare delivery.

- Evaluate the adequacy of underlying knowledge from nursing science, related fields, and professional foundations as it informs nursing practice.

- Demonstrate competence in the development of inquiry relevant to practice, education, or administration.

I gained knowledge and confidence in evaluating academic and clinical performance in nursing and healthcare. As I have done activities such as analyzing a variety of assessment procedures for use in academic nursing education and nursing professional development. I also have done activities in summarizing social and legal issues impacting evaluation of educational outcome achievement, and analyzing methods used to evaluate achievement of learning and program outcomes. I became knowledgeable in applying program planning and evaluation principles, including cost-benefit analysis and clinical outcome measures, to evaluate educational program effectiveness. I am confident to critically analyze the educational practices as the basis for evaluating, revising, and improving the nursing and healthcare curricula. I also know how to interpret the relationship among elements in a curriculum and be able to apply principles of curriculum development in planning a curricular design for an identified problem. As a leader in healthcare delivery, these skills will help me prepare to deal with ever-changing trends in the field of nursing and healthcare because I will be able to evaluate the clinical performance at the largest Psychiatric hospital in Washington State.

Relationship of Both Courses to My Practice and the Curriculum Goals

The University of Washington Tacoma Leadership Master's level curriculum goals include the following:

1. Gain competencies in leadership behaviors.

2. Develop skills related to human and fiscal resource management.

3. Develop skills related to health care management, evaluation, and the ethics of health care systems and organizations.

4. Gain competencies in clinical outcomes management.

5. Evaluate policies that relate to healthcare delivery.

6. Develop skills in the use and evaluation of technology in health care environments.

I am the oldest woman in my original family of seven girls. I had to help my mom a lot in cooking, cleaning, and caring for my younger brothers and sisters. It is innate for me to set an example and act responsibly in everything I do. Now, let me discuss my current job.

I am currently working at the largest Psychiatric Hospital in a charge nurse position. In this facility, my job as a charge nurse is to lead the entire ward: nursing staff, institutional counselors, and psychology associates. For the nursing staff, I schedule, assign, and delegate tasks. I have to make a quick decision to assign certain tasks such as 1:1 therapeutic monitoring, suicidal risk monitoring, seclusion, and restraint. I also have to assign nursing staff for meal monitoring for those patients who have chronic and acute medical conditions such as critical diabetes, a risk for dehydration, and an inability to feed themselves. When incidents happen, such as when a patient falls, assaults, altercations, and injuries, such as wounds and bruises, I have to write an incident report. I have to collaborate with my treatment teams, such as the nursing supervisor, administrator, psychologist, psychiatrist, medical, and social workers. Whatever situation arises, such as a patient may be needing to transfer to the emergency department or just in the ward treatment for intravenous fluids and catheterization, I am responsible for carrying out doctor's orders and other interprofessional team recommendations. I communicate with physicians and multidisciplinary team members through the proper utilization of Situation, Background, Assessment, Recommendation (AHRQ, 2018). I communicate with the treatment team regarding patients' previous and present conditions, medication updates, laboratory works, treatment planning, and addendums, as well as patient leaves, appointments, and family visits. As a charge nurse, I am responsible for maintaining the peace and order of the entire ward through effective communication and collaboration among the treatment team and the interprofessional team (AHRQ, 2018).

As a charge nurse, I must supervise and delegate tasks to colleagues (licensed nurses and nursing aides) within their scope of practice and follow up on feedback in order to interpret patient information and make critical decisions about what intervention is necessary. Nursing care is implemented according to the care plan so that the continuity of care for the patient during hospitalization and in preparation for discharge needs to be assured. The care plan includes data, diagnoses, and treatment goals (ANA, 2018), and the whole care team has access to the care plan (AHRQ, 2018). Both the patient's status and the effectiveness of the nursing care must be continuously evaluated, and the care plan modified as needed. In order for nursing care to be effective, research for evidence-based practice should be conducted in support of improving practice and patient health outcomes (ANA, 2018; and AHRQ, 2018).

My team is composed of psychiatrists, psychologists, administrators, nurses' staff, and social workers. Each of the team members has a very important role and function. In every day's meeting, we make plans and determine objectives. In my team, it is vital that everyone shares a common purpose, vision, and values, which are vital for formulating a treatment plan (Marshall & Broome, 2017; and Maccoby et al., 2013).

There are several challenges in my leadership role, and I will discuss how the courses I took equip my abilities to address these challenges.

The first challenge is staff shortage. For example, the majority of nursing staff in my unit are float nurses or temporary staff who do not know the patients. In my experience, safety concerns arise mostly when there is not enough regular staff on the ward. I have confidence that I can manage this through effective communication and providing orientation.

The second challenge is that the nature of my workplace is very dynamic and diverse; it always has newly hired nurses and other nursing staff coming in for training. All newly hired nurses have different backgrounds, experiences, and learning styles. After completing the course T NURS 512, I know how to develop an individualized mentoring plan. In addition, the newly hired nurses might experience some power struggles with senior staff, and this might cause conflicts. In order to promote anti-bullying at my workplace, I support, respect, and care for all the members of my team. This way, I am also modeling a culture of a great team and demonstrating a work environment that is free of intimidation and abusive behaviors (MacLean, Coombs, & Breda, 2016; Edmonson, & Bolick, 2017).

Having the humility and compassion to serve my patients and colleagues, as well as being responsive to the policies, rules, and regulations of my organization is one of my strengths that makes me a successful leader (Marshall & Broome, 2017).

Application to Master's Essential IX (Master's Level Nursing Practice)

"Essential IX: Master's – level nursing graduates must have an advanced level of understanding of nursing and relevant sciences as well as the ability to integrate this knowledge into practice" (American Association of Colleges of Nursing [AACN], 2018).

I care about my job, and I care about my patients. They are the reasons why I am pursuing the master's program in leadership in healthcare delivery at the University of Washington Tacoma. I have been applying what I learned in the program in my practice. I am eager to offer my competencies in leadership in healthcare delivery at my workplace at Largest Psychiatric Hospital. Currently, I am actively planning to improve patient care by utilizing evidence-based practice, theories, and different theorists' perspectives in making individualized treatment plans for my patients, providing guidance for my workforce, specifically the nursing staff and the newly hired RNs, and actively improving nursing work environment by utilizing what I have learned from these two courses TEDUC 502 and T NURS 512.

Overall, I believe that there is no such thing as a perfect leadership style. I am a situational – transformational – strategic leader. A situational leader is flexible in every situation that arises. This is an important leadership style in my workplace, which is a psychiatric facility because situations can be very unpredictable when dealing with psychiatric patients and multicultural staffs (Marshall & Broome, 2017). Transformational leader aims and works to obtain an exemplary result – "a role model for trust"

(Marshall & Broome, 2017, p. 15). A strategic leader utilizes different perspectives from other scholars and evidence-based practices in making vision, mission, goal, and objectives. A strategic leader is a leader who defines purpose and vision and aligns people, processes, and practical values in support of the organizational purpose (Marshall & Broome, 2017; and Maccoby et al., 2013).

References

Agency for Health care Research and Quality [AHRQ] (2018). National Quality Measures Clearinghouse is a public resource for summaries of evidence-based quality measures and measure sets. NQMC also hosts the HHS Measures Inventory. Retrieved from

https://www.qualitymeasures.ahrq.gov/

American Nurses Association (ANA) (2018). The nursing process. Retrieved from:

http://www.nursingworld.org/EspeciallyForYou/What-is-Nursing/Tools-You-Need/Thenursingprocess.html

American Association of Colleges of Nursing's (AACN) (2018). *Essentials of Master's Education in Nursing.* Retrieved from: http://www.aacn.nche.edu/education-resources/essential-series

Edmonson, C., Bolick, B., & Lee, J. (2017). A moral imperative for nurse leaders: Addressing incivility and bullying in health care. *Nurse Leader, 15*(1), 40-44.

Keating, S., & Zuccarini, M. (2015). *Curriculum development and evaluation in nursing* (3rd ed.). New York, New York: Springer Publishing Company.

Maccoby, M., Norman, C. L., Norman, C. J., Margolies, R. (2013). *Transforming health care*. Hoboken: Wiley.

MacLean, L., Coombs, C., & Breda, K. (2016). Unprofessional workplace conduct, defining and defusing it. *Nursing Management, 47*(9), 30-34.

Marshall, E., & Broome, M. (2017). *Transformational leadership in nursing: From expert clinician to influential leader* (Second ed.). New York, NY: Springer Publishing Company.

Mesner-Andolšek, D., & Šumi, R. (2017). *The integrity of the servant leader*. Abingdon, Oxon; New York, NY: Routledge.

Reflection

Maricel Long, RN

University of Washington-Tacoma

Course Option

2018

Identify strategies for leading quality improvement within a local hospital

1. Relational strategies of leadership.

Decision-makers cannot hope to develop and implement new strategies for quality without properly engaging healthcare providers, communities, and service users. Healthcare providers need to operate within an appropriate policy environment for quality and with a proper understanding of the needs and expectations of those they serve in order to deliver the best results. Moreover, communities and service users need to influence both quality policy and the way in which health services are provided to them if they are to improve their own health outcomes.

As a leader in healthcare delivery, I must support improving teamwork and collaboration between inter-professionals in healthcare delivery. Effective team leaders organize the team, identify and articulate clear goals and each member's responsibilities, communicate changes and follow-ups, and encourage team members to collaborate. Effective team members enable conflict resolution in a learning environment and model effective teamwork—teamwork that offers a powerful solution to improving collaboration and communication. Effective communication is a necessary skill to build an effective and efficient team, which is essential in preventing and alleviating errors that cause injury and harm to patients. The result is high-quality health care outcomes.

As a leader in healthcare delivery, it is vital to know how to get along well with other team members – this is a skill necessary to work as a team. This was experienced when I spent time at SC Hospital chatting with my preceptor and having group conferences with other SC Hospital team members, such as the Data Analyst, the Equipment Manager, the intensive care unit manager, and the Budget Manager (other leadership team members). The SC Hospital team members and I were having collaborative activities; we were looking at the Living Our Mission current events, Living Our Mission dashboard and graphics, analyzing the meaning of it. I have always observed leadership strategies with my preceptor through my communication with her and other SC Hospital team members in a professional and respectful manner. I have demonstrated as clear and concise written assignments as possible. I have also critically analyzed the interactions and collaborations between the leadership team members and other professionals in SC Hospital. Effective healthcare systems demand teamwork, a key advantage in safe and quality patient care.

2. Decision-making processes of leadership.

My preceptor's leadership style is a mixture of democratic and transactional. I observed her many times how she deals with people and how she deals with people with transactions. Though she stated that she believes in open communication, she said that she must guard her time.

However, for example, around 11:00 am to 1:00 pm is an open hour for her to welcome any staff to go to her office and talk to her about anything.

While looking at the organizational dashboard and several other bulletin boards in SC Hospital on their floor, specifically in the orthopedic and PCU departments, I can integrate scientific findings with the literature reviewed on PDSA quality improvement and benchmarking. Therefore, as a leader in healthcare delivery, I must be knowledgeable and able to articulate methods, tools, performance measures, and standards related to quality improvement and safety. As a leader in healthcare delivery, I must have enough skills in PowerPoint Excel as a tool to show data in a pictorial form such as pie, graph, bar, column or other charts on the PowerPoint Excel. Overall, I have reviewed policies, PDSA and Deming cycle, dash-boarding (Living Our Mission), skin data, PICO, Triple Aim, and benchmarking. The lesson I have learned is that leaders in healthcare delivery are doing a lot of research and doing the decision making and problem-solving in improving policies, understanding data, and understanding evidence-based practice to improve quality and safety in healthcare.

References

American Nurses Association (ANA) (2017). Nursing

quality. Retrieved from: http://www.nursingworld.org/ncn

(Links to an external site.) Links to an external site.g

Castner, J., Foltz-Ramos, K., Schwartz, D., & Ceravolo, D.

(2012). A leadership challenge: Staff nurse perceptions after

an organizational TeamSTEPPS initiative. The Journal of

Nursing Administration, 42(10), 467-72.

Gittell, Jody Hoffer, Beswick, Joanne, Goldmann, Don, &

Wallack, Stanley S. (2015). Teamwork

methods for accountable care: Relational coordination and

TeamSTEPPS. Health Care Management Review, 40(2),

116-25.

Institute of Healthcare Improvement [IHI](2018).Tool.

Retrieved.http://www.ihi.org/resources/Pages/Tools/PlanD

oStudyActWorksheet.aspx

Institute of Healthcare Improvement [IHI] (2018). IHI triple

aim initiative. Better care for individuals, better health for the populations, and lower per capita costs. Retrieved from.http://www.ihi.org/Engage/Initiatives/TripleAim/Pages/default.aspx

Sherwood, G., & Barnsteiner, J. (2012). Quality and Safety in nursing: A competency approach to improving outcomes (2nd ed.). Chichester, UK: Wiley-Blackwell

The W. Edward Deming Institute (2018). Deming 101: Theory of knowledge and the PDSA improvement and learning cycle. Retrieved from:

https://blog.deming.org/2013/12/deming-101-theory-of-knowledge-and-the-pdsa-improvement-and-learning-cycle/

Independent Study

Leader in Healthcare Delivery

Independent Study

by

Maricel Long, RN

2018

Abstract

In traditional education, the teacher leads the class from the front, whereas in advanced teaching, the teacher serves as a facilitator who encourages the class to think and ask questions. It encourages everyone to participate and to speak up. In this way, the teacher's attention is on everybody, and the teacher will be able to determine the student's weaknesses and strengths so that a plan can be made for the student for a better grasp of learning. Advanced education is a pedagogical association which values experience over learning facts at the expense of understanding what is being taught. Advanced education thinking embraces the idea that we should teach students how to think and that a test cannot measure whether a student is an educated person. Although there are some laws which prescribe what material should be covered, flexibility in meeting the needs of each student's learning style must be considered. This paper is an independent study of the books of Hooks, 1994 and Keating,

2015. This is one of the requirements for the culminating paper.

Keywords: curriculum development, teaching and learning, learning theories, nursing curriculum.

Teaching, Curriculum Development and Evaluation in Nursing

"While the world order, the national society, and the healthcare system change so rapidly, it is difficult to predict the future; there are prevailing trends that should have an impact on the development and evaluation of nursing curricula over the next decade" (Keating, 2015 p. 376,)

According to Keating (2015), it is the responsibility of a leader to continually assess/monitor the curriculum to maintain its integrity, which is implemented through an instructional process such as theory classes, laboratory practice, and clinical experience. An identification of beliefs about learning and teaching processes is the first step in curriculum development. Nursing leaders (educators) hold the ultimate responsibility for curriculum development. Nursing leaders (educators) must agree on their beliefs about the learning processes their students have to undergo to master the knowledge and skills necessary for competent and caring nurses. The major theories, concepts, and models serve to guide leaders and educators in developing mission and philosophy statements to create a program and build a curriculum plan. These also will guide leaders or educators in the implementation of the curriculum through the process of instructional designs and strategies and in evaluating students. The curriculum development must consider a collaborative approach from different curriculum experts' planners in discussing how learning best occurs. Through these, guidance on the consistency among goals, course objectives, assessment, and evaluation is maintained. Learning outcomes demonstrate whether the goals and objectives have been met, which provide feedback on the educational processes (Keating, 2015).

According to Hooks (1994), educators must acknowledge any effort to transform institutions that reflect a multicultural stance. According to Hooks (1994), "To teach in a manner that respects and cares for the souls of our students is essential if we are to provide the necessary conditions where learning can most deeply and intimately begin" (p. 13). Hooks (1994) discussed multicultural education where there is no social equality. Teachers to promote a classroom where there is no racism, sexism, sexist oppression, class exploitation and culture of domination. Hooks (1994) discussed a change in the educational systems: teaching in a multicultural world, building a multicultural education, and creating a curriculum based on "multiple ways and multiple references" (p 36). Hooks (1994) emphasized collaboration and dialogue among leaders (educators) in creating the best teaching and learning practices, recognising the value of individual voice and everyone's existence. According to Keating (2015), diversity is not only in terms of race, ethnicity, culture, language, and gender but also in terms of the diversity of opportunities in nursing. Nursing care requires cultural sensitivity and awareness of differences among groups, while cultural competence denotes the knowledge and skills required for delivering care in cross-cultural situations (Keating, 2015).

According to Keating (2015), leaders or educators must be flexible in their teaching style per students' needs. The learning theories, education taxonomies, and the application of critical thinking to evidence-based practice are vital to curriculum development. Learning theories provide guidance in dealing with each student's learning. Teaching critical thinking to students is vital to be able to respond to the ever-changing needs and trends in healthcare delivery. The graduates' professional performance provides a critical measurement of the educational program. Students, their families, nurse educators, staff in the practice setting, the patients receiving nursing care from students and graduates, and the overall healthcare system utilize its graduates to answer the complexity of healthcare delivery. Nurses must be prepared to provide leadership in the management of healthcare services and to address policy issues. Nurses, as being the most ethical of professions, must be involved in the key healthcare groups such as advisory and governing boards and work with coalitions of consumers, politicians, and professionals.

According to Hooks (1994), "It is crucial that critical thinkers, who want to change our teaching practices, talk to one another, collaborate in a discussion that crosses boundaries and creates a space for interventions" (p.129). According to Keating (2015), inter-professional communication and collaboration are necessary for the discussion and planning of the educational program in order to answer the needs of the complexity of the current U.S. healthcare system. Professionalism, professional values, and nursing practice: theories and ethics (the core and the American Nurses Association (ANA) code of ethics) are essential documents and recommended standards for education at the various levels of professional nursing practice.

The Different Theories and Theorists' Perspectives

The Behaviorist model in which the teacher's role as the transmitter of knowledge is one theory to be considered. However, leaders must consider other different theorists' perspectives in order to be effective in impacting students learning. The application of this principle is reward and punishment in the classroom and clinical setting. Behavior reinforcement through reward and punishment increases the likelihood of that behavior being repeated (Keating, 2015). The social cognitive theory emphasizes the importance of the interaction among personal characteristics, behaviors, and the social environment. Learning occurs through observation of the environment or role modeling. Personal beliefs such as self-efficacy are important contributions to this perspective, which provides the foundation for powerful teaching strategies that strengthen persistence and effort.

Role modeling and other kinds of observational learning provide common and influential teaching strategies relevant to nursing students (Keating, 2015). The Cognitivism view focuses attention on internal mental processes such as thinking, memory, information processing, and information organization. This perspective suggests many strategies for presenting content in ways that foster memory and understanding for a learner (Keating, 2015). The Constructivist perspective assumes that learners construct their own version of what they learn and understand. That means that learners produce knowledge based on their beliefs and experience, and social interactions are a critical aspect of this process. This perspective argues for teaching content from multiple perspectives and providing real-life problems in all their complexity and realism. Apprenticeships, in which learners work in authentic situations with experts, and problem-based learning are two strategies supported by this approach since they embrace complex situations, perhaps with more than one good approach (Keating, 2015).

Definition of Terms

According to Keating (2015), conceptual models and theories provide the foundation for curricular content and pedagogical innovations. Learning theories pre-exist in technologies and electronic educational materials such as in online courses. Time, empirical research, and thoughtful discussion will determine whether traditional theories remain relevant to tomorrow's classrooms and academic issues and whether new paradigms will emerge. A newer paradigm may be necessary in order to continue to use traditional models. Learning theories remind planners about the importance of complex content, challenging cognitive tasks, self-efficacy, professional role modeling, information organization, and regard for students. These theories help provide counteracting upward pressure for faculty to design appropriately challenging yet practical curricula for today's healthcare practitioners (Keating, 2015).

A curriculum is a formal plan of study that provides the philosophical underpinnings, goals, and guidelines for the delivery of a specific educational program. The classic components of a nursing curriculum include the mission and vision, philosophy, purpose, framework, objectives or student learning outcomes (SLOs), and an overall implementation plan. Curriculum development needs to recognize continuous monitoring of the program, at least annually, to ensure that it is meeting the original mission, framework, goals, and objectives of the curriculum. Curriculum changes are based on the feedback from students, faculty, and consumers; faculty's individual interpretations of the course content and changes in personnel, setting and/or expansion in nursing knowledge. In order to meet the healthcare demand, it is necessary to revise as appropriate to respond to the ever-changing needs of the healthcare system. A curriculum plan provides guidelines for a specific educational program to be implemented (Keating, 2015). The overall purpose of curriculum development is to meet the learners' needs by ensuring that it meets educational and professional standards and that it is responsive to the current and future demands of the healthcare system (Keating, 2015).

The philosophy for a curriculum should flow from the mission and vision as it gives faculty members the opportunity to discuss the flow of the mission and vision. It gives faculty members the opportunity to discuss their beliefs, values, and attitudes about nursing and education which imparts a body of knowledge and skills for the next generation of care providers (Keating, 2015). The mission and vision statements serve as the guiding documents for developing long-range goals and implementing them. Measures to determine if the mission is realized throughout the educational process and according to the expectations of graduates' performance in the real world, give feedback as to how well the mission is met. A cost analysis of the budget is needed for the amount allotted to the various functions of the program that support the mission. Academic and infrastructure support systems are analyzed for congruency with the mission (Keating, 2015).

Quality healthcare and patient safety are concepts that are embedded in nursing knowledge and clinical practice based on the recommendations of the ION (2001) regarding patient safety. Quality healthcare and patient safety concepts are receiving an increased emphasis in the education of health professionals and the diversity of healthcare. Increased acuity levels and patients with complex physiological and psychological challenges add to the challenges of providing safe and quality care. With effective and efficient interdisciplinary and inter-professional collaboration, quality healthcare and patient safety are within reach. The result is a safe and compassionate healthcare environment (Keating, 2015).

Conclusion

I believe that teaching and learning have to be flexible as each student is unique and has different experiences or situations in life. It is important to consider all learning theories, concepts, and theorist perspectives. However, I believe that there are more factors to be considered in education approaches, such as the learner's socioeconomic status, preferences, environmental condition, as well as physical, emotional or psychological well-being.

Figure 1: Concept Map of Curriculum Development

By: Maricel Long, RN

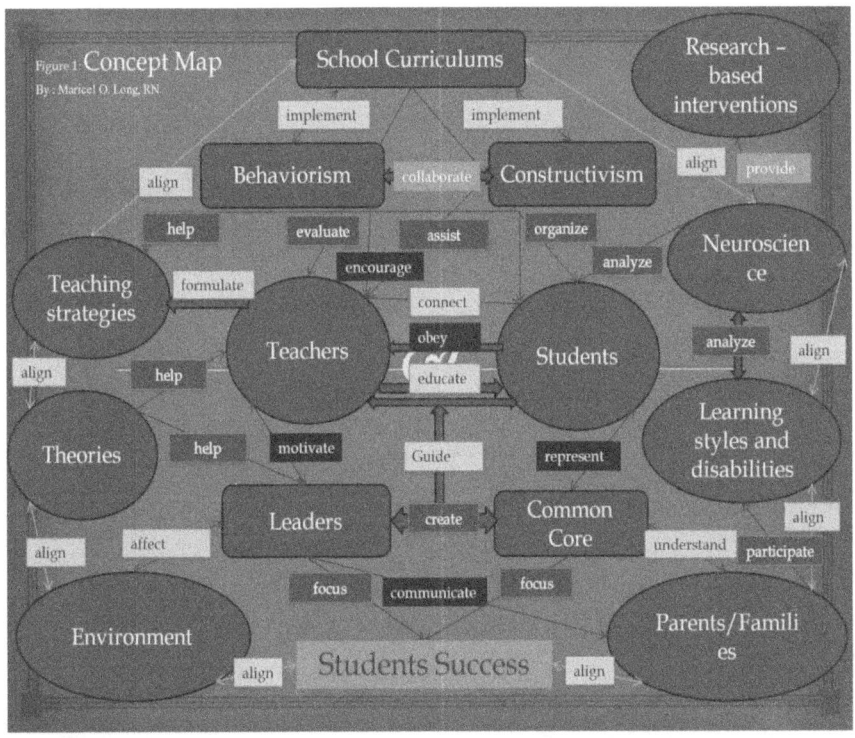

References

Hooks, bell. (1994). *Teaching to transgress: Education as the practice of freedom*. New York: Routledge.

Keating, S. (2015). *CURRICULUM DEVELOPMENT AND EVALUATION IN NURSING* (3rd ed.). Springer Publishing Company.

Leader in Healthcare Delivery

Culminating Paper –Work experience

by

Maricel Long

2018

The purpose of this paper is to describe my leadership style by reflecting on two key work experiences. One was when I was working as a Chef Assistant at Happy Home, followed by my current workplace as a Charge Nurse at Largest Psychiatric Hospital. In this paper, I will at least provide one leadership challenge I came across at each job with references from the literature.

First Job Description

When I was 17 years old, I started serving at an orphanage home currently known as Happy Home. I was serving the missionary people and church people, where I stayed for 6 years.

During those years, while I was at Happy Home, I cooked and served food for missionaries, acted as a chef assistant, as well as did housekeeping jobs. My main task was to cook and serve breakfast for missionaries and church people, including the pastor and other church members. During the weekend, I would cook lunch and dinner, too, when the chef wanted to take a rest or do some personal errands. While I was on this job, I usually had to wake up very early in the morning, go to the market to buy food items, prepare, cook, and serve the food to the missionaries.

The Challenge

The missionaries would wake up very early every morning at 05:30 AM to do praise and worship, which they called "morning praise." At that time, my greatest challenge as a teenager was to rise earlier than the missionaries in the morning. I had to get up very early in the morning in order to be able to buy fresh and affordable foods (fruits, eggs, milk, and bread) from the Agora, the public market, and attend morning praise whenever possible.

My Strength

While working for the orphanage, I learned to take responsibility and work with gratitude, knowing that I was serving very important people: the missionaries. They were the people hailing from different countries such as England, Norway, Sweden, Poland, Switzerland, and America, which helped me learn about the different cultures as I got to observe different languages and styles, especially eating habits and foods. Due to this experience, I learned the importance of spiritual health and humility. I learned that a leader does not have to be rigid to be successful in leading. As the Golden Rule stated, "Do unto others as you would have them do to you" (Mesner-Andolšek, & Šumi, 2017, p. 29). One influential leader and writer, John Maxwell, "understands the golden rule as an effective leading principle of integrity in every situation" (Šumi et al., 2017, p. 29). Integrity reflects a healthy organization as it reflects how the workers behave, express their opinions and values, and how the leader creates a kind of work environment climate (Edmonson, & Bolick, 2017) that is free of intimidation and bullying. Both ethical and moral standards are necessary for the success and existence of an organization and the success of a leader (Šumi et al., 2017). Now, let me discuss my current job.

Second Job Description

My current job is as a Registered Nurse (RN). I am currently working at Largest Psychiatric Hospital in a charge nurse position. In this facility, I was initially taking care of geriatric patients who were chronically and gravelly disabled in both medical and psychiatric conditions at the Psychiatric Recovery Center ward (Recover Centre ward), largest Psychiatric Hospital, for about 9 months. Later, I moved to the admission ward through administrative transfer to do admission for psychiatric mentally ill patients. I did this admission job for over one year as a Charge nurse. Now, I am currently in a PRP-type ward; PRP stands for Psychosocial Rehabilitation Program using Social Learning Principles for patients who are recovering from chronic mental illness. PRP wards emphasize reinforcement of positive behavior and role modeling. I have been in this PRP ward as the charge nurse for one and a half years. Overall, I have been working at largest Psychiatric Hospital as a charge nurse for three years and seven months.

Basically, my job as a charge nurse is to lead the entire ward over nursing staff: Scheduling, assigning and delegating tasks to staff. Most of the times, I have to make a quick decision to assign certain tasks such as 1:1 therapeutic monitoring, suicidal risk monitoring, seclusion, and restraint. I also have to assign nursing staff for meal monitoring for those patients who have chronic and acute medical conditions such as critical diabetes, a risk for dehydration, and an inability to feed themselves. When incidents happen, such as when a patient falls, assaults, altercations, and obtain injuries such as wounds and bruises, I have to do an incident report. I have to collaborate with my treatment teams, such as the nursing supervisor, administrator, psychologist, psychiatrist, medical, and social worker. Whatever situation arises, such as patients needing a transfer to the emergency department or just in the ward treatment for intravenous fluids and catheterization, I am responsible for carrying out doctor's orders and other interprofessional team recommendations. I have a collaborative work environment and teamwork. I communicate with physicians and multidisciplinary team members through the proper utilization of situation, background, assessment, and recommendation SBAR (AHRQ, 2018). I communicate with the treatment team regarding patients' previous and present conditions, medication updates, laboratory works, treatment planning, and addendums, as well as patient leaves, appointments, and family visits. As a charge nurse, I am responsible for maintaining the peace and order of the entire ward through effective communication and collaboration among the treatment team and the interprofessional team (AHRQ, 2018).

As a charge nurse, I facilitate to promote and restore client health by implementing the nursing process as a means for delivering holistic and patient-focused care (American Nurses Association [ANA] (2018). In order to do this, I must communicate effectively to the physicians and multidisciplinary team members through the proper utilization of SBAR (Agency for Healthcare Research and Quality [AHRQ], 2018). As a charge nurse, I am expected to provide education to both the client and the family members regarding acute and chronic conditions (ANA, 2018). I must review the patient data in order to make critical decisions when creating a plan of action. Using measurable, realistic, and achievable goals, I will be able to produce individualized short-term as well as long-term goals with interventions that may incorporate physiological, psychological, sociocultural, spiritual, economic and lifestyle factors to promote wellness and recovery (ANA, 2018).

As a charge nurse, I must supervise and delegate tasks to colleagues (licensed nurses and nursing aides) within their scope of practice and follow up on feedback in order to interpret patient information and make critical decisions about what intervention is necessary. Nursing care is implemented according to the care plan so that the continuity of care for the patient during hospitalization and in preparation for discharge needs to be assured. Care is documented in the patient's record. Assessment data, diagnosis, and goals are written in the patient's care plan (ANA, 2018) so that nurses and other inter-multidisciplinary teams caring for the patient have access to it (AHRQ, 2018). Both the patient's status and the effectiveness of the nursing care must be continuously evaluated, and the care plan modified as needed. Research should be conducted in support of improving practice and patient health outcomes (ANA, 2018; and (AHRQ, 2018).

Nursing depends on teams to carry out its mission and objectives. Nurses stay in jobs where teamwork is effective. Effective teams are highly productive and make fewer errors

(AHRQ, 2018; Gaston, Short, Ralyea, & Casterline, 2016; Kalisch, Weaver, and Salas, 2009; and Vertino, 2014). My team is composed of Psychiatrists, Medical, Psychologists, Administrators, Nurses/ Nursing staff, and Social Workers. Each of the team members has a very important role and function. Every day, my team meets for about an hour or two, depending on how many cases and issues we are trying to discuss in a conference meeting. This is where we learned each other's contribution to patient care. This is when we make plans and objectives on what to do next. These collaborative activities can be challenging in a way. If one does not cooperate, then the others have to compromise, or else there will be a conflict in patient care. On my team, it is vital that everyone has to share a common purpose, vision, and values, and it is evident through treatment plan formulations of patient care and everyday goal charting (Marshall & Broome, 2017; and Maccoby et al., 2013).

The Challenge

The **first challenge** in this job is short staffing. For example, when almost all of my nursing staff were floats or on calls especially never been and do not know the patients. No matter how busy it can be on my shift, I have to orient them in order for them to know what to expect with patient care and maintain the ward milieu as acceptable as possible. I had confidence in myself that I could manage my job; I managed it through hard work and effective communication by orienting floats and on-call staff, no matter how busy I was. These kinds of staffing issues would also drain the charge nurse's energy and time just to keep the staff updated on what has to be done. In my experience, safety concerns arise mostly when there are not enough regular staff on the ward.

The **second challenge** is that the nature of my workplace is very dynamic and diverse; it always has newly hired nurses coming in for training. Some of these newly hired nurses are not so new; some have 10 years or more experience from outside hospitals, and some are actually novices. All newly hired nurses have different styles of learning behaviors. I learned to work or train them in many different places. For example, one trainee may want to take charge right away, and another one wants to delay and prepare more. On the other hand, some want to focus on knowing the chart while others prefer to learn the online stuff or online way of learning about work. Some want to interact with patients right away, and some do not—they prefer to learn through all the paperwork first before taking the actual rounds on the floor. There are power struggles experienced among new hires against senior staff (everyone wants to be the boss), which can cause conflict. Power struggles can cause substantial conflict and can be difficult to handle. In order to promote anti-bullying at my workplace, I supported a just culture by building rapport, giving out respect, and caring for others. This way, I am also creating a culture of a great team and a work environment that is free of intimidation and abusive behaviors (MacLean, Coombs, & Breda, 2016; Edmonson, & Bolick, 2017).

The Strength

The one strength I discovered as a leader is that I have a big heart; I have the humility and compassion to serve my patients and colleagues, as well as being responsive to the policies, rules, and regulations of my organization. This strength puts me in balance toward being a successful leader and a compassionate one. I am not working just to take care of my patients alone; I am also a nurse to myself (making sure my overall health and well-being are maintained to an optimum level so that I am able to help others) (Marshall & Broome, 2017); I am nurse to my colleagues, and responsive to my organization's policies, rules, and regulations.

My Leadership Style

Overall, I believe that there is no such thing as a perfect leadership style. I am a situational – transformational – strategic leader. A situational leader is flexible in every situation that arises. This is an important leadership style in my workplace, a psychiatric facility, as situations can be very unpredictable when dealing with psychiatric patients and multicultural staff (Marshall & Broome, 2017). Transformational leader aims and works to obtain an exemplary result – "a role model for trust" (Marshall & Broome, 2017, p. 15). A strategic leader utilizes different perspectives from other scholars and evidence-based practices in making vision, mission, goal, and objectives. A strategic leader is a leader who defines purpose and vision and aligns people, processes, and practical values in support of the organizational purpose (Marshall & Broome, 2017; and Maccoby et al., 2013).

Reference

Agency for Health care Research and Quality [AHRQ] (2018). National Quality Measures Clearinghouse is a public resource for summaries of evidence-based quality measures and measure sets. NQMC also hosts the HHS Measures Inventory.

Retrieved from https://www.qualitymeasures.ahrq.gov/

American Nurses Association (ANA) (2018). The nursing process.

Retrieved from:

http://www.nursingworld.org/EspeciallyForYou/What-is-Nursing/Tools-You-Need/Thenursingprocess.html

Castner, J., Foltz-Ramos, K., Schwartz, D., & Ceravolo, D. (2012). A leadership challenge: Staff nurse perceptions after an organizational TeamSTEPPS initiative. *The Journal of Nursing Administration, 42*(10), 467-72.

Edmonson, C., & Bolick, B. (2017). A moral imperative for nurse leaders. Nurse Leader, 15(1), 40-44.

Foltin, A., & Keller, R. (2012). Leading change with emotional intelligence. Nursing Management, 43, 11, 20-5.

Gaston, T., Short, N., Ralyea, C., & Casterline, G. (2016). Promoting Patient Safety: Results of a TeamSTEPPS® Initiative. The Journal of Nursing Administration, 46(4), 201-7.

Kalisch, B. J., Weaver, S. J., & Salas, E. (2009). What does nursing teamwork look like? A qualitative study. Journal of Nursing Care Quality, 24, 4.

Maccoby, M., Norman, C. L., Norman, C. J., Margolies, R. (2013). Transforming health care. Hoboken: Wiley.

MacLean, L., Coombs, C., & Breda, K. (2016). Unprofessional workplace conduct. Nursing Management, 47(9), 30-34.

Marshall, E., & Broome, Marion. (2017). *Transformational leadership in nursing: From expert clinician to influential leader* (Second ed.). New York, NY: Springer Publishing Company.

Mesner-Andolšek, D., & Šumi, Robert. (2017). *The integrity of the servant leader*. Abingdon, Oxon; New York, NY: Routledge.

Vertino, K. (2014). Evaluation of a TeamSTEPPS© initiative on staff attitudes toward teamwork. *The Journal of Nursing Administration, 44*(2), 97-102.

My Six-Month Leadership Trial at the Largest

Psychiatric Hospital

Located in the Western Washington, United State

The Executive Summary

Maricel Long, RN-MN (RN3)

2019

I am thankful to all managers for giving me support when I needed them. I am especially thankful to my manager, whose name I can't mention for privacy purposes. He personally told me, "Thank you for helping us; you really got hired because you are good." This feedback had a great impact on me as a leader; it has given me a sense of assurance that I was doing good at my job as a nursing supervisor and that I was on the right path towards improving my leadership experience and abilities. The manager lead, whom I, again, cannot mention the name for privacy purposes. She also told me, "You are doing good," and said, "You are a day shift material. You move to the day shift after 6 months." I was an evening shift nursing supervisor then. This was good feedback as well and she was letting me know that I am going in the right direction with my leading and managing skills. Several managers had told me I was doing good, and they appreciated me as an addition to the team. When I was going through conflict, one manager looked me in the eye and said, "Your team is a priority," a simple eye gesture like this is leadership wisdom, and a simple word that made me feel supported and a sense of connection to her as one of my managers. All of these have impacted me positively and catapulted me toward success in my six-month leadership trial.

How I was doing during the first 4 weeks of Orientation to my New Role as nursing supervisor.

I tried my best to learn. I worked with floor staff and multidisciplinary teams such as Nurses, Therapists, Social workers, and Doctors to understand how they do things here in the Community Program ward. I am especially grateful to one nursing supervisor (I can't mention her name for privacy) who finally helped me and treated me very well. She showed me the entire building, toured me around to all wards, and kept introducing me as a new nursing supervisor to the multidisciplinary team, and managers. She also taught me how to do staffing as part of my daily responsibility as a nursing supervisor. I am also thankful for several staff members while I was on training. Another supervisor taught me the daily routine and the culture and climate of this new work environment, including staff issues, patients' statuses and concerns and conflicts. The two co supervisors who were scheduled to orient me on the ward went on vacation. I had to find other ways to get myself oriented, especially since I had never been to this area and program called the Community Program (CP) ward at the largest Psychiatric Hospital in Western Washington.

Anyway, these 6 months of leadership trial was not a hunky dory. I met some nursing supervisors who were eating their young (arrogant and a bully). However, my humility and compassion for my co-workers and patients made it easier for me to compromise, work it out as a team and be included. That being said, "Respect is earned," I kept in mind that in leadership, there are moments when I must agree to disagree in order to work things out....and I succeeded. Team building, indeed, has different layers.

There are layers of conflict –this is to clarify expectations (what they expect of me and what I expect of them), and sometimes, it can be lengthy. What I wrote is actually "just the tip of the iceberg."

My experience with my supervised staff during the First 6 months of leadership trial

There were many incidents during these 6 months trial period. Right when I started my new position, I got the news that one of my supervised staff is on temporary reassignment for a misconduct case; he is going to get fired soon because of many issues and misconduct that were investigated, and the result was substantiated. Three months later, another one of my supervised staff was placed on temporary reassignment due to an accusation of harassment and was being investigated for it. A month after that, another incident happened. One of my supervised staff was arrested during work hours at the workplace/facility ground due to accusations of felony and misdemeanor domestic violence cases, which turned out to be the most devastating experience for my entire supervised staff. It also shook the entire ward team. This incident was very emotional for both patients and staff. Our community program patient happened to observe the situation as they were able to go to their ground privileges, saw the police cars and saw one of their caregivers being arrested on the facility ground. For a few days, some of the staff lost some sleep over this incident. Both patients and staff were asking, "What's going on? What's happening to this staff?" For a few days, I observed patients go to bed earlier than usual, and the ward got quieter. They were going through something, I guess. This staff got cleared after over a year of the investigative process, etc…She got cleared and returned to work with us.

All nursing task:

1. Start with Scheduler: Putting staff on schedule/ assigning staff, including printing patient movement forms and inter-shift report papers in preparation for TT meeting.

2. Inter-shift Report

3. Shift Begins: RN first rounds from wall to wall to check all patients and staff, including checking out VS, BS, Labs, Appt. and Medical Transports.

4. Active treatment groups/patients

5. Start Acuity

6. TT conference (Report)

7. RN follow-ups/updates cache

8. Finalizing Assessments and chartings

9. PRNs/med reconciliation

10. End of shift Inter-shift report

- ✓ Observing and recording patients' behavior

- ✓ Coordinating with physicians and other healthcare professionals for creating and evaluating customized care plans

- ✓ Analyzing patient's symptoms and taking required actions for his/her recovery

- ✓ Maintaining reports of patients' medical histories and monitoring changes in their condition

- ✓ Directing and supervising LPNs and CNAs

- ✓ Checking the stock on a regular basis to maintain the inventory level and placing orders if required

- ✓ Adhering to the protocols, norms, rules and regulations in order to maintain complete medical records

✓ Maintaining a hygienic and safe working environment in compliance with healthcare procedures

✓ Providing instant care during medical emergencies, like car accidents, burns, heart attacks and strokes

✓ Discussing treatment with pharmacists and physicians in critical cases

Other Nursing duties:

✓ Feed, bathe and dress patients.

✓ Take patient vital signs.

✓ Serve meals, make beds and keep rooms clean.

✓ Set up medical equipment and assist with some medical procedures.

✓ Answer calls for help and observe changes in a patient's condition or behavior.

✓ Respond immediately to calls from patients for assistance or treatment and alert medical staff to pending emergency situations.

✓ Encourage all residents to get exercise and participate in scheduled activities.

✓ Engage in housekeeping tasks such as replacing linens on beds, cleaning patient rooms and removing and replacing trash bags.

✓ Work with dining room personnel to ensure that all residents get the correct meals and that all residents are able to eat.

Non-patient care duties that take up time by nursing

✓ Leave tracker

✓ Mechanics such as printer rebooting

✓ Empty laundry

✓ Taking trash

✓ Cleaning

✓ PRNs purple book

- ✓ LMS

- ✓ Escort to yard/boundary walks/

AL/community outings

- ✓ Open packages

Strategic Plan

Maricel O. Long, RN

I believe that everyone can learn (staff and patients)-it is just a matter of how we give instructions. Let's emphasize that from the beginning to the end of each day, we are here to care, and our role is to do no harm.

2019

(Updated from 2017)

My current organization is the largest Psychiatric Hospital located in Western Washington, United States. The processes that have been designed and redesigned within the system are the revisions of policies and procedures. Reinforcement of these policies and procedures has been very challenging in my current organization at present. The information is disseminated through our bulletin board online (intranet) to which everyone has access. My team is composed of Psychiatrists, Medical, Psychologists, administrators, nurses/ nursing staff, and social workers. Each of the team members has a very important role and function. Every day, my team meets for about an hour or two, depending on how many cases and issues we are trying to discuss. This is where we learned each other's contribution to patient care. This is when we make plans and objectives on what to do next. This can be challenging in that if one does not cooperate, then the others have to compromise, or there will be a conflict in patient care. On my team, it is vital that every one shares a common purpose, vision, and values, and it is evident through treatment plan formulations of patient care and everyday goal charting (Maccoby et al., 2013).

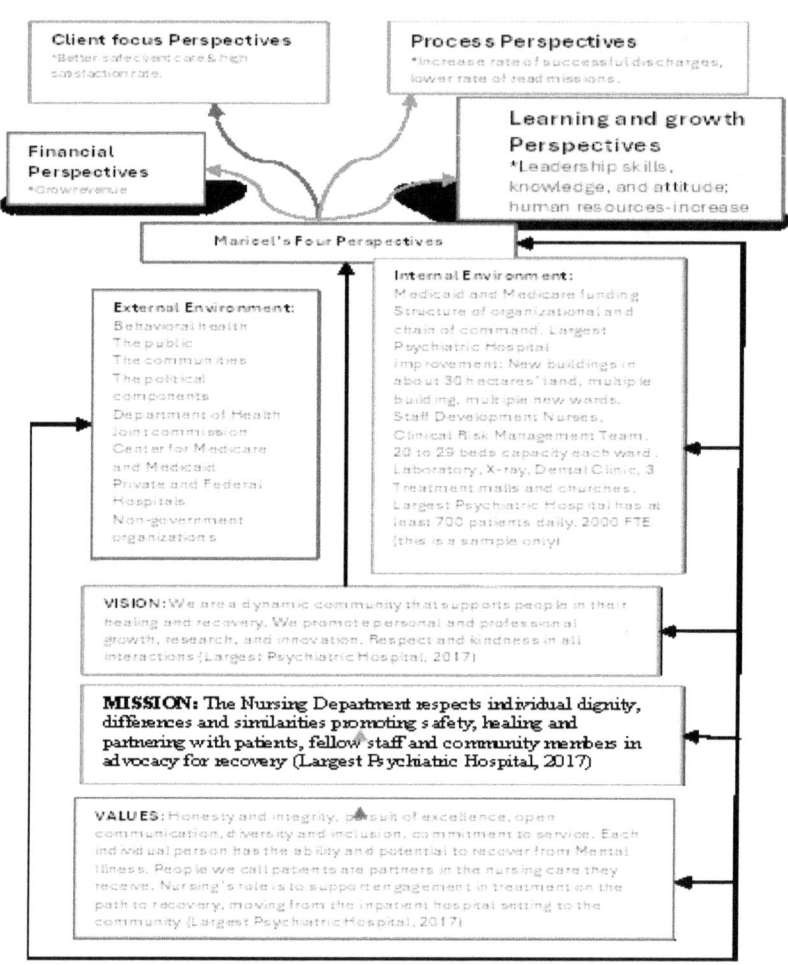

Figure 1. Maricel's Strategic Leadership and Management Model

Maricel's Strategic Leadership and Management Model - Analysis

After all the class discussions, lectures, and PowerPoint presentations, including Maccoby et al. (2013) and the discussion on "Crossing the quality chasm" and looking at my current organization, I am able to create this strategic leadership and management Model framework. Starting at the very bottom; the first box of the framework is the values since values play a very important part to this writer. As a leader/manager, values tell us how the staff or employees are expected to behave toward each other, toward clients, toward suppliers/stakeholders and toward the community (Carla R., 2016; Maccoby et al., 2013; Largest Psychiatric Hospital, 2017).

In the Largest Psychiatric Hospital, the Charge nurse plays a big role in molding staff's behavior. They are responsible for instilling values in staff—a role model. If the Charge nurses comply with the values, Largest Psychiatric

Hospital's top management view of the kind of company they are trying to create will be successful. Therefore, I put values as the foundation for creating a strategic leadership and management model because it is the one that helps to define the company and differentiate it from other companies (Carla R., 2016; Maccoby et al., 2013; and Largest Psychiatric Hospital, 2017).

The second box is the Mission, and the third box is the Vision. The Mission is very important to be remembered in creating strategic leadership and management model because it is the reason why the organization exists. It provides a clear view of what the company is trying to accomplish. It specifies the client served, the needs satisfied or values received by the client and the technology used. The Vision is the top management view of the kind of company it is trying to create and where the company will be in the future (Carla R., 2016; Maccoby et al., 2013; and Largest Psychiatric Hospital, 2017).

The Internal and External Environment: External environment analysis consists of examining the internal environment to identify opportunities and threats like, for example, stakeholders' market, technology advances and competitors. Internal environment analysis is an assessment of the organizational strengths and weaknesses, quantity and quality of resources available to the organizations, such as financial, capital, technology and human resources (Carla R., 2016; Maccoby et al., 2013; and Largest Psychiatric Hospital, 2017).

Both the external and internal environment of an organization must be analyzed to create a SWOT analysis necessary to create strategic perspectives. Therefore, after assessing the external and internal environment of the Largest Psychiatric Hospital and with my experience as charge nurse for over 4 years at Largest Psychiatric Hospital, I am able to create strategic leadership and management Model with 4 perspectives, which are shown in the above figure (strategic leadership and management Model), the four boxes on the top: 1.) financial perspective, which to grow revenue or save money; 2.) client-focused perspectives, which to have better-safe care & high satisfaction rate; more discharges and reduced readmissions; 3.) Process perspective, which has an increased rate of successful discharges and lower rate of readmissions; 4.). Learning and growth perspective, which is composed of good leadership skills, knowledge, attitude, and with consideration of the resources: man, money and machinery within the organization. The strategic perspectives really consist of answering questions on how to achieve the mission and vision (how to achieve the goals) (Carla R., 2016; Maccoby et al., 2013; and Largest Psychiatric Hospital, 2017).

Having proper tools, strategic intelligence leadership and collaboration among leaders all throughout organizations is the solution to health care improvement. It is important that changes in practices reach every level of care, from leader to

patient. Perfect care may be a long way off, but much better

care is within our grasp. Taking advantage of new

information technologies will be an important catalyst to

moving us beyond where we are today. Through structural

and educational changes that are enforced in each

department and level of healthcare organizations, we can

achieve optimal healthcare. The result is a safer, more

efficient, cost-effective system that better satisfies patients

and health care workers. Nonetheless, these changes must be

created by, enacted upon, and taught both traditionally and

by example by healthcare leaders (Carla R., 2016; Maccoby

et al., 2013; Institute of Medicine. Committee on Quality of

Health Care in America, 2001; and Largest Psychiatric

Hospital, 2017).

References

Carla R. (2016). Strategic plan 2015-2017: Behavioral

health administration. Washington State Department of

Social & Health Services.

Institute of Medicine. Committee on Quality of Health Care

in America. (2001). *Crossing the quality chasm: A new*

health system for the 21st century (Quality chasm series).

Washington, D.C.: National Academy Press.

Maccoby, M., Norman, C. L., Norman, C. J., Margolies, R.

(2013). *Transforming health care: A system guide to*

improve patient care, decrease costs, and improve

population health (1st ed.). Hoboken, New Jersey: Jossey-

Bass.

Largest Psychiatric Hospital (2017). Quality assessment &

performance improvement plan 2016-*2018. Washington*

State Department of Social & Health Services.

Inter-Professional Collaboration

Maricel Long, RN

University of Washington-Tacoma

Quality and Safety

2018

Quality and safety remain a serious concern, with expected outcomes not being achieved and wide variations in standards of healthcare delivery within and between healthcare systems. Improved quality outcomes are not, however, delivered by health service providers alone. Communities and service users are the co-producers of health. They have critical roles and responsibilities in identifying their own needs and preferences and in managing their own health with appropriate support from health service providers. While it is important to recognize these differences in roles and responsibilities, it is equally important to recognize the connections between them. Decision-makers cannot hope to develop and implement new strategies for quality without properly engaging health service providers, communities, and service users. Healthcare providers need to operate within an appropriate policy environment for quality and with a proper understanding of the needs and expectations of those they serve in order to deliver the best results. Communities and

service users need to influence both quality policy and the

way in which health services are provided to them if they are

to improve their own health outcomes. TeamSTEPPS is an

advanced program that works to solidify collaboration

among the healthcare team to achieve the best outcomes for

patients (Agency for Healthcare Research and Quality

[AHRQ] 2018; American Nurses Association (ANA) 2017;

and Sherwood & Barnsteiner, 2012). The purpose of this

paper is to describe and analyze TeamSTEPPS as an

effective tool to improve communication among

interprofessional teams.

The TeamSTEPPS (Team Strategies and Tools to

Enhance Performance and Patient Safety) is an evidence-

based framework to optimize team performance across

healthcare delivery. This program was developed by the

Agency of Healthcare Research (AHRQ) and the

Department of Defense to improve patient safety by guiding

healthcare organization's efforts to increase collaboration and communication among healthcare professionals. TeamSTEPPS is a curriculum that offers ready-to-use curricula and specialty modules for office-based care providers, long-term care settings, and rapid response teams. TeamSTEPPS 2.0 Core Curriculum has three main modules: Essentials course, fundamentals, and supplemental. It focuses on five key principles which are based on team structure and four teachable-learnable skills such as communication, leadership, situation, monitoring, and mutual support. It has three-way arrows, which are dynamic interplay between the four skills and the team-related outcomes. Interaction between the outcomes and skills is the basis of a team striving to deliver safe, quality care and support quality improvement. Encompassing the four skills is the team structure of the patient care team, which represents not only the patient and direct caregivers but also

those who play a supportive role within the healthcare
delivery system (AHRQ, 2018).

AHRQ is interested in learning how better teamwork can
improve diagnosis and prevent diagnostic errors. Since
healthcare systems are shifting to value-based purchasing
systems (pay for quality of service), AHRQ has been
continuing to support research that evaluates the importance
of teamwork, communication, and coordination in safety and
quality, and how to efficiently support effective healthcare
teams. TeamSTEPPS foster teamwork and collaboration,
which protect the patient's safety, and help to improve the
quality of care that the patient is receiving. Facilities that
identify low levels of communication and teamwork can
clearly benefit from access to TeamSTEPPS curricula as it
serves as a model to support safe, accurately diagnose
patients through healthcare teams that work across different
healthcare settings (AHRQ, 2018; and Sherwood &
Barnsteiner, 2012).

One way to support teamSTEPPS is by the utilization of the Situation, Background, Assessment, and Recommendation (SBAR), which has been used nationwide for effective communication. Safe and efficient care involves the coordinated activities of a multi-team system through effective communication. The SBAR is a technique for communicating critical information that requires immediate attention and action concerning a patient's condition. Through the utilization of this tool, nurses can send out messages to inter-professional team members about patients' acute and chronic conditions.

As master-prepared RNs, we have to support improvement in a teamwork setting and continue to collaborate between inter-professionals in how delivering healthcare is implemented in order to achieve quality outcomes. Effective leaders create a goal and objectives, encourage equal responsibility and task assignments, provide feedback when necessary, and encourage team members to help one another and model effective teamwork.

Effective leaders utilize evidence-based tools to promote

teamwork, which offers a powerful solution to improving

collaboration and communication within the institution

(AHRQ, 2018).

Gittell, Beswick, Goldmann, Wallack, & Stanley (2015)

discussed relational coordination as an effective multilevel

teamwork measure that enhances TeamSTEPPS, which is an

effective multilevel teamwork intervention. According to

Gittell et al. (2015) TeamSTEPPS can be used by healthcare

systems to respond to challenges in healthcare by identifying

areas of improvement of teamwork with consideration to

shared knowledge and timely communication among

interprofessional teams. Gaston, Short, Ralyea, & Casterline

(2016) defined teamwork as an essential component of

communication in a safety-oriented culture. Poor

communication is a persistent patient safety hazard, and

human errors related to communication failures are the cause of most adverse events. Hence, a well-designed system must be in place to prevent and detect errors, as well as reduce harm when a mistake occurs. Gaston et al. (2016) aim their study to design, implement, and evaluate a modified TeamSTEPPS training program by incorporating coaching and focus groups in order to improve staff perception of teamwork and communication in clinical practice. Results showed that staff perception of teamwork and communication improved after the implementation of the TeamSTEPPS program. Gaston et al. (2016) concluded that TeamSTEPPS is a practical, effective, and low-cost patient safety endeavor. Effective teams are more productive and less stressed workers, which produce higher quality care, fewer errors, and better patient satisfaction.

Castner, Foltz-Ramos, Schwartz, & Ceravolo (2012) defined teamwork as an essential part for patient safety in healthcare organizations and nursing teams. Caster stated that organizational development should support effective teamwork, which comprises teaching and training the necessary skills to build teamwork, leadership engagement, and teamwork training with a focus on a just culture. Castner et al. (2012) applied their study of the TeamSTEPPS teamwork training to bedside RNs with the aim to improve RN perceptions of leadership. The initiatives were to align the perspectives and teamwork efforts of leaders and bedside nurses, which indicated that charge nurses should be involved in the design.

Vertino (2014) modified the TeamSTEPPS training initiative to improve the attitudes of nursing staff toward teamwork in an inpatient hospital unit. Their analysis revealed a significant increase in total scores as well as statistical significance on all 5 components of teamwork, including team structure, leadership, situation monitoring, mutual support, and communication. The data supports that TeamSTEPPS training can be useful in promoting improved attitudes toward teamwork. Therefore, highly functioning teams make fewer errors, which are obtained through

teamwork.

Conclusion

Effective healthcare systems demand teamwork, a key to

safe and quality patient care. Teamwork can transform the

culture in healthcare to safe, efficient, cost-effective, high-

quality delivery. However, effective communication is s

necessary skill to build collaborative teams, which is

essential in preventing and alleviating errors that cause

injury and harm to patients. Changes in practices and

infrastructures must reach every level of care, from leader to

patient. Having proper tools, strategic intelligence

leadership, teamwork and collaboration among leaders all

throughout the organization is the solution to safety and

quality healthcare delivery. Through structural and

educational changes that are enforced in each department

and level of health care organization, we can achieve optimal

health care. The result is a safer, more efficient, cost-effective system that better satisfies patients and health care

workers.

Reference

Agency for Health care Research and Quality [AHRQ]

(2018). National Quality Measures Clearinghouse is a

public resource for summaries of evidence-based quality

measures and measure sets. NQMC also hosts the HHS

Measures Inventory. Retrieved

formhttps://www.qualitymeasures.ahrq.gov/

American Nurses Association (ANA) (2017). Nursing

quality. Retrieved

from: http://www.nursingworld.org/ncn (Links to an

external site.)Links to an external site.g

Castner, J., Foltz-Ramos, K., Schwartz, D., & Ceravolo, D.

(2012). A leadership challenge: Staff nurse perceptions

after an organizational TeamSTEPPS initiative. *The

Journal of Nursing Administration, 42*(10), 467-72.

Gaston, T., Short, N., Ralyea, C., & Casterline, G. (2016).

Promoting Patient Safety: Results of a TeamSTEPPS®

Initiative. *The Journal of Nursing Administration, 46*(4), 201-7.

Gittell, Jody Hoffer, Beswick, Joanne, Goldmann, Don, & Wallack, Stanley S. (2015). Teamwork methods for accountable care: Relational coordination and TeamSTEPPS. Health Care Management Review, 40(2), 116-25.

Sherwood, G., & Barnsteiner, J. (2012). Quality and Safety in nursing: A competency approach to improving outcomes (2nd ed.). Chichester, UK: Wiley-Blackwell

Vertino, K. (2014). Evaluation of a TeamSTEPPS© initiative on staff attitudes toward teamwork. *The Journal of Nursing Administration, 44*(2), 97-102.

PRN PAIN MEDICATIONS AND THE NURSING PROTOCOL AT THE LARGEST PSYCHIATRIC HOSPITAL LOCATED IN WESTERN WASHINGTON, UNITED STATES, PSYCHIATRIC RECOVERY CENTER

by

Maricel Long, RN

A SCHOLARLY PROJECT PROPOSAL

SUBMITTED IN PARTIAL FULFILLMENT

OF THE REQUIREMENTS FOR THE DEGREE

OF

MASTER OF NURSING

In Leadership in Healthcare Delivery under the

supervision of

Sharon Gavin Fought, PhD, RN

UNIVERSITY OF WASHINGTON-TACOMA

May 2017

Chapter 1: Problem Statement

The purpose of this chapter is to state the problem, its incidence or frequency, and why it is important to nursing. This chapter ends with a statement of the purpose of the proposed project. The focus of this scholarly inquiry is related to the use of Pro re nata (PRN) pain medications for psychiatric patients at one adult psychiatric facility, Largest Psychiatric Hospital, and Recover Center wards.

PRN medications are typically not given on a set schedule, but are prescribed to address a target symptom, and are intended to be given as the symptom arises and discontinued once the symptom subsides" (Largest Psychiatric Hospital procedural manual, 2017). Registered Nurses' (RN's) assessment and authorization prior to giving the PRN pain medications are necessary per protocol. In March 2017, the Largest Psychiatric Hospital director of nursing services sent a Policy Memo stating that all RNs must assess the patient prior to authorizing PRN medications. Licensed Practical Nurses (LPNs) are no longer allowed to give medications without the RN's assessment of the patient and authorization for the LPN to give a PRN medication. According to the Largest Psychiatric Hospital Policy memo (2017), the effectiveness of the PRN medication must also be documented.

The LPNs will document the pre- (rating) scale in the MediMAR, the electronic medical record where it provides a pain scale of 0-10; however, it is the RN's responsibility to assess the effectiveness of the PRN medications. The RNs will chart the effectiveness of the PRN in the MediMAR as follows: minimal improvement, moderate improvement, no adverse reactions or symptoms noted, no change noted/reported, other-, please provide an explanation below, PRN effective, and patient asleep-no signs/symptoms of pain. (State of Washington Department of Social and Health Services, Largest Psychiatric Hospital, Medication Policy Manual, 2017). This is a new regulation implemented for all

RNs at Largest Psychiatric Hospital, and it is not yet known if all RNs and LPNs adhere to this policy memo and/or medication administration policy.

According to this writer's queries, during monthly audits of MediMAR, the Largest Psychiatric Hospital administration found the following issues: one patient was noted receiving 120 PRNs in one month, another patient was in severe pain but was not reported to the RN; an RN did not assess the patient and has only been given Tylenol 650 mg PO every four hours PRN few times. Then, an emergency of life and death happened (the patient almost died due to severe pain) –the patient survived, but the administration was alarmed. Finally, according to this writer's queries, many PRNs were not documented during monthly PRN audits.

According to four other RNs (this writer is not included), one supervisor, and one psychiatrist at Largest Psychiatric Hospital, Recover Center wards, it was implemented due to the results of the Center of Medicaid and Medicare (CMS) survey. Therefore, it is important to comply with this Policy memo or lose funding due to nurses not doing their job—that is why it is important to nursing.

If this proposed project is undertaken, nursing assessment data will be collected, and an analysis of whether or not the RN complied with the protocol and/or the Largest Psychiatric Hospital policy on giving PRN pain medications will be conducted and published.

To all nurses at Largest Psychiatric Hospital, Recover Center wards: This study will help increase awareness of the outcomes based on the data gathered at Largest Psychiatric Hospital, Recover Center wards. This study will highly benefit nurses mainly because it could be a medium in determining proper, utmost and efficient care for adult psychiatric patients who are in pain and will give Newly hired nurses at Largest Psychiatric Hospital and Recover Center wards information on how to properly do nursing assessment on adult Psychiatric patients.

To future researchers: This study may serve as a baseline for future studies and as a reference.

Therefore, the purpose of this proposed project is to review 100 charts with documentation of PRN pain medication administration in the RECOVER CENTER wards to determine if RN's complied or did not comply with the rules/policy around the administration of PRN medications that were implemented for all RN's at Largest Psychiatric Hospital, Recover Center wards.

Chapter 2: Review of Literature and Theoretical Framework

The purpose of this chapter is to introduce concepts/theories, review the literature, and then discuss the literature related to each concept.

The PRN process in psychiatric wards is complicated and potentially allows nurses to use their clinical judgement regarding the administration of PRN Medications prescribed by doctors. The proper use of PRN by nurses depends on several factors, including clinical settings, preference for medication, relationship with doctors, nursing experience, nursing technique, and working environment (Fujita, Nishida, Sakata, Noda, and Ito, 2013). According to Largest Psychiatric Hospital policy 6.10 issued May 2017, "the RN will perform a pain assessment and, if indicated, refer to the physician for a comprehensive assessment." According to the Largest Psychiatric Hospital policy 6.10 issued May 2017, reassess any intervention for a complaint of pain and document the effectiveness of the treatment within one hour". Therefore, it is clear that it is being implemented that the RN has to do a pain assessment at Largest Psychiatric Hospital.

Nursing assessment: Nursing assessment is the identification by a nurse of the needs, preferences, and abilities of a patient that are vital start to a caring relationship. Assessment includes an interview with and observation of a patient by the nurse and considers the symptoms and signs of the condition, the patient's verbal and nonverbal communication, the patient's medical and social history, and any other information available.

Among the physical aspects assessed are vital signs, skin color and condition, motor and sensory nerve function, nutrition, rest, sleep, activity, elimination, and consciousness. Among the social and emotional factors included in the assessment are religion, occupation, attitude toward hospital and health care, mood, emotional tone, and family ties and responsibilities. Assessment is extremely important because it provides the scientific basis for a complete nursing care plan. Good clinical practice requires periodic reassessment of patient's use of PRN medication (Largest Psychiatric Hospital Medication Policy Manual, 2017).

Mental illness refers to a wide range of mental health conditions and disorders that affect your mood, thinking and behavior. Examples of mental illness include depression, anxiety disorders, schizophrenia, eating disorders and addictive behaviors. Many people have mental health concerns from time to time. Mental and behavioral disorders cannot be adequately addressed unless the individual is as free as possible from physical distress, including pain. Patients with dementia, Schizophrenia, and other cognitive disorders may not be able to describe their pain, may not perceive the pain, or may express it indirectly in assaultiveness, agitation and/or withdrawal. Pain is defined by the patient rather than by the staff. When a patient is complaining of pain or observed by any staff member to be experiencing physical pain, that observation is to be reported to a ward RN and/or physician. An intervention for a complaint of pain will be reassessed and documented for effectiveness on the PRN. Chemically dependent patients may require additional assessment, closer monitoring and more patient, family and healthcare provider education. Still, the goals and treatment elements are the same as for any non-chemical dependent patient (Largest Psychiatric Hospital Policy Manual, Pain Assessment and Management, revised December 2010, 2017). Nurses can expand their existing role, continuing to make contributions to health care within the modern model by developing its foundational caring-healing and health strengths that have always been present on the margin."

Baker, Lovell, & Harris (2008) studied using a pre-post exploratory design with two acute mental health wards in the

NW of England to determine the impact and acceptability of a good practice manual on prescribing and administration practices of PRN psychotropic medication in acute mental health wards. Over the total trial period of 10 weeks, 28 of 35 patients received 484 doses of PRN. Patients had a mean of 3.6 prescriptions of 14 different PRN medications in 34 different dose combinations prescribed. Medication errors beyond poor quality of prescribing occurred in 23 of the 35 patients (65.7%). Prescription quality improved following the introduction of the intervention, but the quality of nursing notes was reduced. The manual's acceptance by both nursing and medical staff was high. The introduction of the manual appeared to influence some of the practices associated with the prescribing and administration of PRN psychotropic medications. Further, larger, more robust studies are required in this area. In particular, research is required to identify the reasons why professionals continue to rely so heavily on using PRN medication.

Douglas-Hall & Whicher (2015) reviewed the required medication to determine whether it is good clinical practice or not when compared to the same drug given regularly to people with schizophrenia who are in the hospital. Douglas-Hall & Whicher (2015) found no trials that could be included in the review. Although the practice of using medication as required is common, there is currently no good evidence as to whether this is the best way of helping people when compared to them being given a regular dose of the same medication. Douglas-Hall & Whicher (2015) independently inspected abstracts and papers for inclusion. Douglas-Hall & Whicher (2015) stated, "If trials had been found, we would have extracted data from the papers and quality assessed the data. For dichotomous data, we would calculate the risk ratios (RR) with 95% confidence intervals (CI). We would have conducted analyses on an intention-to-treat basis. If data were available, we would have completed a 'Summary of findings' table using GRADE."

Zhao, Sampson, Xia, and Jayaram (2015) assessed the efficacy of brief psychoeducational interventions as a means of helping severely mentally ill people when added to standard care, compared with the efficacy of standard care alone. Zhao et al. (2015) included twenty studies with a total number of 2337 participants in this review. Nineteen studies compared brief psychoeducation with routine care or conventional delivery of information. One study compared brief psychoeducation with cognitive behavior therapy. Based on information from a limited number of studies, brief psychoeducation does seem to reduce relapse and encourage people to take their medication. Those receiving brief psychoeducation also have more favorable results for mental state and social functioning. It is suggested that insight into the illness can help people understand the need for treatment and subsequently improve the prognosis. However, the nature of schizophrenia is such that it alters people's thought processes, and they are often unable to have insight into their illness.

Medication is an important component in the palliative, symptomatic, and curative treatment of many diseases and conditions. However, improper or incorrect dose of medication administration causes great harm if it is administered to the patient. Therefore, hospitals need to develop an effective and safe medication management system that addresses an organization's medication processes, such as storage, preparation and dispensing, administration, monitoring, and evaluation, to eliminate any potential harm to patients. Also, it is equally important that multiple disciplines work together closely to have effective and safe medication management. The medication management standards address activities involving various individuals within an organization's medication management system, such as licensed practitioners and staff. A well-implemented medication management system supports patient safety and improves the quality of care

(Largest Psychiatric Hospital Pharmacy and Therapeutic Committee).

A PRN pain medication is usually written on the drug chart by the clinician so that nurses can administer it at their discretion and in the doctor's absence. Any regimen of medication administered for the short-term relief of behavioral disturbance or psychotic symptoms is to be given at the discretion of ward staff as required with fixed non-discretionary patterns of drug administration of the same drug(s). It is very common for as-required drugs to be given to patients with schizophrenia in order for them to feel comfortable while they wait for their long-term treatments to take effect. If not properly monitored, this treatment method can result in many negative consequences, such as negative drug interactions or toxic levels of certain chemicals found in behavioral drugs monitoring and thought needs to be put into the treatment of mentally ill patients (Douglas-Hall & Whicher, 2015). Accordingly, PRN medications are typically not given on a set schedule, but are prescribed to address a target symptom, and is intended to be given as the symptom arises and discontinued once the symptom subsides" (Largest Psychiatric Hospital procedural manual, 2017. According to Largest Psychiatric Hospital Medication Policy Manual 70:03, RN must follow the guidelines and must take note of charting the reason for PRN medication and its effectiveness on the MAR.

Therefore, the purpose of this study is to review 100 charts for PRN medications that were given to patients at Largest Psychiatric Hospital, Recover Center to see if Nurses complied or did not comply with the rules/Policies that were implemented for all RN at Largest Psychiatric Hospital, Recover Center wards.

In order to review the effectiveness of the protocol on RN assessments prior to giving PRN pain medications, Donabedian's (1988) quality care model will be used (figure 1). Donabedian develops the framework for measuring quality by assessing elements of structure or process with proven connections to key outcomes of interest. The three Donabedian approaches to assessment are Structure, Process, and Outcomes. Quality- "Quality Assessment Performance Improvement (QAPI) provides oversight of specific areas which directly lead to hospital compliance with CMS and other accrediting body regulations. QAPI is an infrastructure that provides monitoring of the full range of Largest Psychiatric Hospital services for quality of care and safety" (Largest Psychiatric Hospital, QAPI, 2017). Quality is ultimately determined by the degree to which health care improves important patient outcomes.

Structure: "Structure denotes the attributes of the settings in which care occurs" (Donabedian, 1988, p.1745).

In this study, the Structure includes the Recover Center ward environment, providers such as RN, LPNs, and patients, and the protocol or the Largest Psychiatric Hospital policy on giving PRN pain medications. The PRN process in psychiatric wards is complicated and potentially allows nurses to use their clinical judgement regarding the administration of PRN Medications prescribed by doctors. The proper use of PRN by nurses depends on several factors, including clinical settings, preference for medication, relationship with doctors, nursing experience, nursing technique, and working environment (Fujita, Nishida, Sakata, Noda, and Ito, 2013). Safety-"Patient safety is a hospital-wide priority and integrated throughout the committee and organizational structure. The Patient Care Quality Council (PCQC), a subcommittee of the Executive Leadership Team, overseas patient safety-related data collection and analysis is accomplished through a variety of sources, including the National Patient Safety Goals, occurrence reporting, risk management reporting, infection control process, Core Measures, performance improvement teams and departmental indicators" (Largest Psychiatric Hospital, QAPI, 2017). Safety is ultimately determined by the degree to which health care improves important patient outcomes.

Process: "Process denotes what is actually done in giving and receiving care" (Donabedian, 1988, p.1745). These are the patient's well-being or current mental health status, coping strategies, RN assessment and alternative strategies prior to authorizing giving PRN, giving PRN medications and evaluations of the effectivity of care provided, making chart notes, and the implementation of reinforcement of Largest Psychiatric Hospital policy on giving PRN medications. According to Largest Psychiatric Hospital policy 6.10 issued May 2017, "the RN will perform a pain assessment and, if indicated, refer to the physician for a comprehensive assessment." According to the Largest

Psychiatric Hospital policy 6.10 issued May 2017, reassess any intervention for a complaint of pain and document the effectiveness of the treatment within one hour." Therefore, it is being implemented that the RN has to do pain assessment at Largest Psychiatric Hospital.

Outcome: "Outcome denotes the effect of care on the health status of patients and population" (Donabedian, 1988, p.1745). These are patient satisfaction with the quality of care provided, patient health status, or improvement (Donabedian, 1988). Baker, Lovell, & Harris (2008) studied using a pre-post exploratory design with two acute mental health wards in the NW of England to determine the impact and acceptability of a good practice manual on prescribing and administration practices of PRN psychotropic medication in acute mental health wards. Over the total trial period of 10 weeks, 28 of 35 patients received 484 doses of PRN. Patients had a mean of 3.6 prescriptions of 14 different PRN medications in 34 different dose combinations prescribed. Medication errors beyond poor quality of prescribing occurred in 23 of the 35 patients (65.7%). Prescription quality improved following the introduction of the intervention, but the quality of nursing notes was reduced. The acceptance of the manual by both nursing and medical staff was high. The introduction of the manual appeared to influence some of the practices associated with the prescribing and administration of PRN psychotropic medications. Further, larger, more robust studies are required in this area. In particular, research is required to identify the reasons why professionals continue to rely so heavily on using PRN medication.

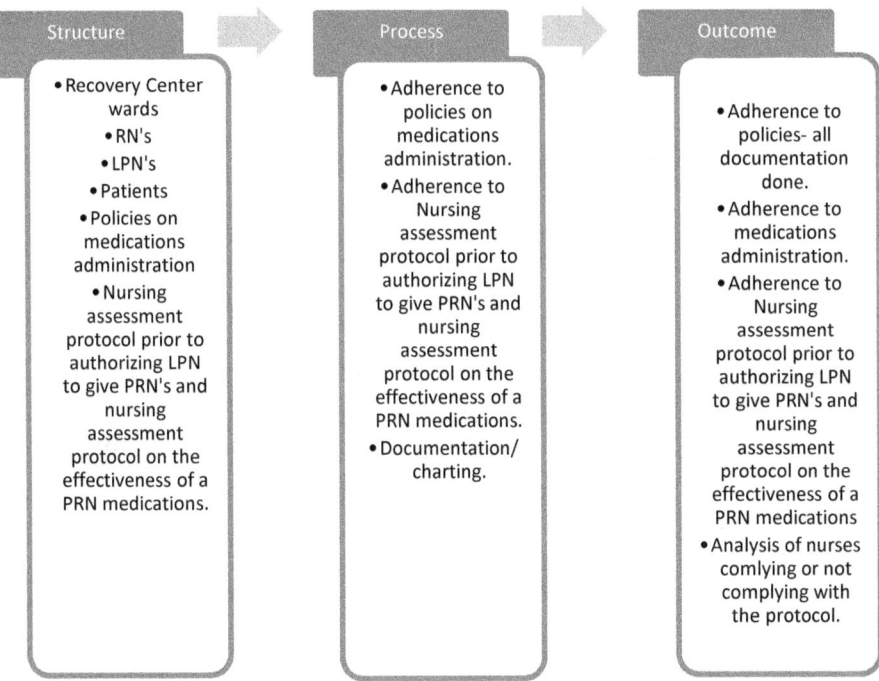

Figure 1. Factors to be considered in reviewing 100 charts for PRN medications were given to the patient to see if Nurses complied or not with the rules/Policies that were implemented for all RN at Largest Psychiatric Hospital and Recover Center wards.

Chapter 3: Methods

The purpose of this chapter is to describe the research design, setting, sample and population, sampling methods, and steps to complete the project.

The researcher will do the following: Conceptualization, review of related literature, analysis of the concept and the review of related literature in order to synthesize and make a summary, designing and planning for the research review and analysis, data gathering, data summary, recommendations, and finally Research writing. The data will be collected through a review of 100 charts, including MediMAR records on PRN medications given to patients at Largest Psychiatric Hospital Recover Center wards and the RN nursing assessment notes on patient charts. The demographic data, such as age, gender, and mental status or diagnosis, will be collected at Largest Psychiatric Hospital Recover Center wards. Protection of human subjects: The patient's name is not included for privacy protection.

Design: Retrospect (retrospective) MediMAR report for 3 months prior to implementation and reinforcement of Largest Psychiatric Hospital policy on giving PRN in March 2017 compared to 3 months after (prospective) the implementation and reinforcement of Largest Psychiatric Hospital policy on giving PRN in March 2017.

Plan of data analysis: The data will be collected through a review of 100 charts-MediMAR records on PRN medications given to patients at Largest Psychiatric Hospital, Recover Center wards, and the RN nursing assessment notes on patient charts. The demographic data, such as age, gender, and mental status or diagnosis, will be collected at Largest Psychiatric Hospital Recover Center wards. Describe and analyze the data differences between 3 months prior to the implementation of the LARGEST PSYCHIATRIC HOSPITAL policy on giving PRN on March 2017 (the patient's data from December 2016 through

February 2017 -will be collected) and 3 months after the implementation of the Largest Psychiatric Hospital policy on giving PRN on March 2017 (the patient's data from May 2017 through July 2017 -will be collected). SPPSS Statistics will be used to run the data collected to do data analysis. The researcher will look for RN chartings of the effectiveness of the PRN used in the MediMAR as follows: minimal improvement, moderate improvement, no adverse reactions or symptoms noted, no change noted/reported, other— please provide an explanation below, PRN effective, patient asleep-no signs/symptoms of pain. Paper MAR progress notes of that nursing assessment were made to the patient prior to authorizing LPN to give PRN, LPN pre-rating scale on MediMAR, and the effectiveness of PRN used on RN assessment after one hour of PRN given. Finally, 100 charts will be reviewed for PRN medications that were given to patients at Largest Psychiatric Hospital, Recover Center to see if Nurses complied or did not comply with the rules/policies that were implemented for all RN at Largest Psychiatric Hospital, Recover Center wards.

Population and sample: 100 charts that meet these criteria: Adult Psychiatric patients on Recover Center wards, Largest Psychiatric Hospital, had given PRN medications for pain and discomfort.

Sampling methods: It is a convenient sampling method. The researcher will pick at least 3 patients in each ward.

Protection of human subjects: The patient's name is not included for privacy protection.

Create a data collection tool

Get expert review of data collection tool; make changes if needed

Get Largest Psychiatric Hospital IRB and UW IRB approval

Get access to 100 charts

Retrieve these data: RN chartings of the effectiveness of the PRN used in the MediMAR as follows: minimal improvement, moderate improvement, no adverse reactions or symptoms noted, no change noted/reported, other- please provide explanation below, PRN effective, patient asleep-no signs/symptoms of pain. Paper MAR progress notes of that nursing assessment were made to the patient prior to authorizing LPN to give PRN, LPN pre-rating scale on MediMAR, and the effectiveness of PRN used on RN assessment after one hour of PRN given.

The specific questions are: For 100 patients PRN at Largest Psychiatric Hospital, Recover Center wards, for 3 months pre and 3 months post-policy implementation. Does the implementation of the Policy make a significant difference in patient condition? Do all RN's comply with the policy-all documentation 100%?

References

Baker, Lovell, & Harris. (2008). The impact of a good practice manual on professional practice associated with psychotropic PRN in acute mental health wards: An exploratory study. International Journal of Nursing Studies, 45(10), 1403-1410.

Barnes, T., & Paton, C. (2011). Antipsychotic Polypharmacy in Schizophrenia. CNS Drugs, 25(5), 383-99.

Clark, L., Colbert, A., Flaskerud, J., Glittenberg, J., Ludwig-Beymer, P., Omeri, A., . . . Zoucha, R. (2010). Chapter 6: Culturally Based Healing and Care Modalities. Journal of Transcultural Nursing, 21(4_suppl), 236S-306S.

Donabedian, A. (1988). The Quality of Care: How Can It Be Assessed? JAMA, 260(12), 1743-1748.

Douglas-Hall, P., & Whicher, E. (2015). 'As required' medication regimens for seriously mentally ill people in hospital. The Cochrane Database of Systematic Reviews, (12), CD003441.

Fujita, J., Nishida, A., Sakata, M., Noda, T., & Ito, H. (2013). Excessive dosing and polypharmacy of antipsychotics caused by pro re nata in agitated patients with schizophrenia. Psychiatry and Clinical Neurosciences, 67(5), 345-351.

Gastmans, C. (1998). Interpersonal relations in nursing: A philosophical-ethical analysis of the work of Hildegard E. Peplau. Journal of Advanced Nursing, 28(6), 1312-1319.

Hagen, Knizek, & Hjelmeland. (2017). Mental Health Nurses' Experiences of Caring for Suicidal Patients in Psychiatric Wards: An Emotional Endeavor. Archives of Psychiatric Nursing, 31(1), 31-37.

Suliman, W., Welmann, E., Omer, T., & Thomas, L. (2009). Applying Watson's nursing theory to assess patient perceptions of being cared for in a multicultural environment. The Journal of Nursing Research : JNR, 17(4), 293-7.

Tanja-Dijkstra, K., & Pieterse, M. (2011). The psychological effects of the physical healthcare environment on healthcare personnel. The Cochrane Database of Systematic Reviews, (1), CD006210.Zhao, S., Sampson, S., Xia, J., & Jayaram, M. (2015). Psychoeducation (brief) for people with serious mental illness. The Cochrane Database of Systematic Reviews, (4), CD010823.

SC Hospital (SCH) Site Skin Team Work Executive Summary

Maricel Long, R.N.

University of Washington-Tacoma

Fieldwork

2018

SC Hospital Site Skin Team Work Executive

Summary and the Communication Flow between

Regional and Site Based Skin Team

The SCH Site Skin Team

- SC Hospital Skin Team created a Skin Team Charter, also known as a site-based skin team – **Beginning of Spring 2018.**

- Members of this team are the skin champions from each of the inpatient units: med tele, orthopedic, and critical care.

- SC champions will serve as the resource for the SCH team to reduce Hospital Acquired Pressure Ulcer (HAP); RN/ charge nurses and CNAs from the day shift and night shift get together with the RN chairperson, quality manager (the main leader of the skin team), the health educator, and all inpatient units' managers in support with this team.

•   This team will assist in decreasing SCH HAPU and help to formulate strategies for improvements.

•   Vision: to reduce HAPU as measured on the Living Our Mission (LOM) dashboard and Skin team presentation.

•   The ultimate goal: decrease HAPU on the LOM dashboard.

•   Hypotheses: capturing stage 1&2 PU during admission can decrease HAPU and, therefore, increase reimbursement.

•   This site-based skin team has been meeting for 5 weeks now on Wednesdays from 9 am to 1 pm.

•   The team discussed issues and reviewed policies to make sure each of the champions' was aware of the policies if they were to give assistance to the entire inpatient unit. These discussions/ meetings serve as their training as champions.

The Team is Constantly Monitoring their Progress

- Week 1 (March 28/2018): SCH Inaugural Skin Team Meeting (introduction of site-based skin team) – the creation of vision, mission, goal, and objectives.

- Week 2 (April 4/2018): Continuation of the creation of vision, mission, goal, and objectives – Site Based Skin Team –team building.

- Week 3 (April 11/2018): Discussion on the creation of the orchid rounding tool and prevalence study, as well as policies review.

- Week 4 (April 18/2018): Topic on assessment and address - continues on Policy review, including addendums and charts review and the initiation of orchid rounding tool creation.

- Week 5 (April 26/2018): Meeting was canceled due to the fire drill activities on the unit.

- Week 6 (May 2/ 2018): Skin team meeting and floor travel to check patients' beds, watched the NDNQI video about pressure ulcers and skin alteration, and floor travel to check patients' beds. The orchid rounding tool was competed and ready to use.

What the Team Learned During these 5 weeks?

- Nutrition foods – Registered Nurses can order this per policy.

- IRIS – everyone can file this but the communication flow is unclear - to find out if IRIS has been done or has not for an incidence of skin alteration.

- Clarified types of wound cream/lotion: Blue for buttocks and orange for an open wound.

- Clarified types of bed mattresses related to HAPU prevention intervention.

- Clarified Charge Nurses, RNs need to take responsibilities to call MD if wound ostomy nurse is not available in order to obtain an order to initiate pressure injury interventions.

- The Braden score is not being effectively used to drive nursing care.

- Positive reinforcement and just-in-time training in a non-punitive way.

Communication Flow between Regional and Site Based Skin Team

Regional Skin Team

- The SCH site-based skin team chairperson attended for the first time and brought concerns from the site champions for clarification.

- During this regional skin team meeting held on April 19, 2018, there were several important points noted:

1. Communication between departments to whom the patients were transferred in regards to positioning. If the patient is from the pre-operative room, intra-operative, and post-operative, the OR nurse, PACU nurse, and in-patient nurse need to communicate with each other for patient positioning and wound or any skin alterations.

2. Pressure injuries that happened within 72 hours after surgery could be related to the surgery.

3. Several tools being used to prevent or reduce HAPU still need validations – they need to be consistent, relevant, and reliable.

4. Positioning diagram to help aid in repositioning the patient.

5. Daily care flow sheet should be utilized as it shows what positioning the patient while in the OR.

6. Since there is a global shortage of wound ostomy nurses, the Charge Nurses and RNs on the floor need to take responsibility for calling the MD if a wound ostomy nurse is not available in order to obtain an order to initiate interventions instead of waiting.

7. One representative raised concerns about HAPU cases – Miscounted.

Recommendation

- The nurse leaders' roles and influences are necessary for the implementation of pressure ulcer prevention interventions so that they will be operationalized at an optimum level (Soban, Kim, Yuan, & Miltner, 2017).

- Proper assessment and documentation are essential to ensure safety and quality nursing care outcomes (Zrelak, Utter, Sadeghi, Cuny, Baron, & Romano, 2013).

- Continue on consistency for all HAPU prevention interventions per policies: The risk assessment tools, strategies to prevent pressure ulcers, policy, committee, staff education, wound care specialists, and the use of performance or performance monitoring incorporated into routine care.

- For miscounted pressure injury cases, I suggest more effort to improve communication between risk management personnel and quality management personnel.

- Information Technology (IT) to create a clear way to communicate IRIS so that the floor staff: RNs, and CNAs will have a clear view of IRIS and to avoid redundancy.

References

CHI Franciscan Health (2018). Assessment: Patient admission assessment and reassessment policy, 951.25 (Policy Stat ID: 1803033)

CHI Franciscan Health (2018). Skin care and pressure ulcer prevention policy (adult inpatient) 961.00 (Policy Stat ID: 3854690)

Soban, L., Kim, L., Yuan, A., & Miltner, R. (2017). Organizational strategies to implement hospital pressure ulcer prevention programs: Findings from a national survey. *Journal of Nursing Management, 25*(6), 457-467.

Zrelak, P., Utter, G., Sadeghi, B., Cuny, J., Baron, R., & Romano, P. (2013). Using the Agency for Healthcare Research and Quality patient safety indicators for targeting nursing quality improvement. *The Journal of Nursing Administration, 43*(10 Suppl), S51-60.

SC Hospital Action Plan to Reduce Hospital

Acquired Pressure Ulcer (HAPU)

Maricel Long, R.N.

University of Washington-Tacoma

Fieldwork

2018

Abstract

Nursing strategies are necessary in order to obtain high-quality and safety patient outcomes (American Nurses Association (ANA), 2017; and Sherwood & Barnsteiner, 2017). Nurses in leadership positions and frontlines of care are necessary for preventing harm to patients and improving patient outcomes. Proper nursing assessment and documentation is an integral part of the success of the entire healthcare quality from admission to discharge (ANA, 2017; and Sherwood & Barnsteiner, 2017). The National Database of Nursing Indicators (NDNQI) data helps the hospital to achieve the highest level of nursing performance by tracking progress. NDNQI is the voice of nurses across America, which provides insights into quality improvement (ANA, 2017). NDNQI data helps the hospital to achieve the highest level of nursing performance by tracking progress. High-quality care is everyone's responsibility, from clinicians to patients; however, quality and safety in healthcare rely on effective nursing strategies (Soban, Kim, Yuan, & Miltner, 2017; Sherwood & Barnsteiner, 2017; ANA, 2017; Reddy et al., 2006; Zrelak et al., 2013). This paper aims to create an Action Plan to optimize the implementation of nursing strategies in order to reduce Hospital Acquired Pressure Ulcers (HAPU). The Action Plan will not be created without the background and evidence of issues necessitating an action to solve (See 'The Action Plan' and 'Logic Model' next pages down).

Background from the Literature Review

It is the third leading cause of death in the US after cancer and cardiovascular disease (Sherwood & Barnsteiner, 2017). Hospital-acquired pressure ulcer (HAPU) cases in stage 1 to stage 4 were documented as 64.30%: Stages 3 to 4 and unstageable were 20.10%; stage 1 was 13.30%; physicians' documentation at discharge were 58%: bedbound patients 49.10%, and intensive care unit was 61.50 %. These measures excluded patients with length of stays of 4 days or less, "patients admitted from nursing homes and other acute care facilities, and patients who are particularly susceptible to pressure ulcers due to paralytic conditions" (Zrelak et al., p. 554, 2013). The Agency for Healthcare Research and Quality (AHRQ) is a federal agency responsible for improving healthcare quality and safety in the U.S. (Agency for Healthcare Research and Quality [AHRQ], 2016). AHRQ has developed a series of health care decision-making and research tools that can be used by program managers, researchers, and others at the Federal, State, and local levels (AHRQ, 2016). AHRQ uses several Safety and Quality Indicators to measure performance in healthcare and to provide perspectives on overall quality of care outcomes (AHRQ, 2016). HAPU is one of the focuses of patient safety indicators (PSIs). PSIs have the potential to help identify areas of concern, monitor the impact of changes in practice, and provide benchmarks for comparisons" (Zrelak, Utter, Sadeghi, Cuny, Baron, & Romano, (2013).

Policy Driven

1. Different ways to show data:

➢ Observer/expected, Numerator/denominator, and Rate

2. Why it is important to understand:

➢ It is important to understand the population, date range, and reason for data in order to be able to compare and contrast the data. Also, to look at the same data with the same timeframes and the same population if it is comparable; if not, then it is non-comparable.

3. How are these differing times, or why there are different time frames

➤ Calendar year: January to December in the same year.

➤ Fiscal year: It depends on the organization.

➤ performance period (ex. Rolling 12 month's data)

4. Skin data:

➤ Sourcing ex. IRIS, Braden Scale, MAR

➤ Population ex. Critical care unit adult patients (high risk for pressure ulcer)

➤ Date sourcing/ date: When was the data collected, and what timeframes?

➤ The purpose of putting data together, for example, is for comparability.

5. How can we improve pressure ulcers in Critical care?

> Multidisciplinary collaboration or collaborative improvement strategies with utilization of evidence-based practice, policy implementation, assessments, and evaluations (see Table 1)

6. Leadership: How are we going to improve pressure ulcers at SC Hospital- Critical care unit?

Table 1: The PICO Model for clinical Questions
P (Patient, Population, or Problem): Critical care adult patients high risk for pressure ulcer. *How would I describe a group of patients similar to mine?*
I (Intervention, Prognostic Factor, or Exposure): Which main intervention, prognostic factor, or exposure am I considering? "*Multifaceted interventional process* that consisted of an *educational session*, a pressure ulcer *checklist*, a *smartphone* application for lesion monitoring and *decision-making* and a *family prevention bundle*" Loudet et al. (2017). Soban et al., 2017 described the presence and operationalization of organizational strategies to support the implementation of pressure ulcer prevention programs across acute care hospitals. ➢ **Nursing interventions**: *risk assessment tools.* ➢ **Organizational strategies:** policy, committee, staff education, wound care specialists, and use of performance or performance monitoring incorporated into routine care. ➢ Results showed that there were high levels of variations noted in how these strategies were operationalized within individual hospitals. ➢ They concluded that there is a need of *consistency, sustainable performance in order for organizational strategies will be operationalized at an optimum level.* ➢ They added that that *the role and influence of nurse leaders* on pressure ulcer prevention program implementation is necessary. According to Lynn article, "In 2011, the Secretary of Veterans Affairs initiated an aspirational goal of *zero hospital-*

acquired pressure ulcers (HAPU) in the VHA", which resulted on the creation and released on VHA Handbook 1180.02 for Pressure Ulcers Prevention. This became the *primary source for guidance on standardization of pressure ulcer prevention* programs within the VHA, including prescribing key responsibilities for leaders and clinicians and outlining necessary elements for pressure ulcer prevention programs.

Reddy et al. (2006) article

- Focus:
  - ➢ *Mobility, nutrition, and skin health.*
- Appropriate strategies: *repositioning, optimizing nutrition, and moisturization* (showed evidence as appropriate strategies)
  - ➢ The use *of support surfaces, mattress overlays on operating tables, and specialized foam and specialized sheepskin overlays as well as q 2 hours turn.*
- Suggested:
  - ➢ There is a need for a well- designed relevant, randomized controlled trials (RCTs), data, cost-effective.
- Reddy systematically reviewed Pressure ulcers in 3 categories: impairments in mobility, nutrition, or skin health.
- Reddy noted that **Pressure Ulcers** are common in a variety of patient settings and are *associated with adverse health outcomes and high treatment costs.*
- Nonpharmacological interventions that provide data on cost-effectiveness for these interventions.
- Maricel (Mix of non-pharmacological and pharmacological interventions)

SC Hospital Skin Care and Pressure Ulcer Prevention Policy (adult inpatient) 961.00

- All patients in acute care services: MS, critical care, peri-operative, and acute rehab.
- Data source: Addendum A, B, C, D, E, F, G, and H.
- Staff responsible for managing the policy: RN (All patient care clinical team members are responsible for PU relief precautions, movement, and skincare.)
- Patient risk factors: Age, immobility, incontinence, sensory deficient, device r/ PU on admission, prior stage 3 and 4 PU, hypo perfusion states, peripheral vascular disease, diabetes, smoking, restraint use, spinal cord injury, palliative care, OR/ER stay, and poor nutritional status.
- Contributing factors: Bony prominences, sustained pressure (ischemic/soft tissue death), Friction, shear, moisture.
- Patient assessment/reassessment: Cephalocaudal including PU risk assessment and detect the present of Pus, focus skin assessment, and **IRIS**. Patient **whom determined as high risk** will be reassessed by a **second RN** or other staff as second set of eyes. Document accordingly all skin integrity alterations.
- All routine assessment is completed within 12 hours: The Braden scale, skin color, texture, temperature, integrity and areas of potential pressure.
- PU or **wound assessment** must include: etiology, location, size, depth, exudates amount, color,

and odor; appearance of wound bed; color: red, yellow, black, and condition of surrounding skin. • <u>Braden score of less than **18**</u> or alteration of skin integrity must be evaluated by an RN. • Document: picture, date/time, location of wound, and staff signature-place in EHR. • Follow up with MD.
C (Comparison or Intervention as appropriate) Compare before and after *What is the main alternative to compare with the intervention?*
O (outcome you would like to measure or achieve): Reliable outcome or staff and patient satisfaction. Better or worse *What can I hope to accomplish measure, improve, or affect?*

In order to prevent pressure ulcers, SC Hospital created a Pressure Ulcer Prevention Policy for adult inpatients. The policy is intended for all patients in the acute care unit: Medical/surgical, critical care, peri-operative, and acute rehab. Examples of data sources are the Braden scale and Incident report (IRIS). The main staff responsible for this policy is the registered nurse (RN). Other staff or clinical team members are responsible for pressure ulcer precaution, movement, and skin care. Patient risk factors are age, immobility, incontinence, sensory deficient, device-related pressure on admission, prior stage 3 and stage 4 pressure ulcer, hypo-perfusion states, peripheral vascular disease, diabetes, smoking, restraint use, spinal cord injury, palliative care, operating room and emergency department stay, and poor nutritional status. Contributing factors are bony prominences, sustained pressure (ischemic/soft tissue death), friction, shear, and moisture. Patient assessment/reassessment is Cephalocaudal, including pressure ulcer risk assessment. Patients who are determined as high risk for pressure ulcers will be reassessed by a second RN or other staff as the second set of eyes. Finally, all routine assessments are completed within 12 hours, including the Braden scale, skin color, texture, temperature, integrity, and areas of potential pressure. Pressure ulcer or wound assessment must include etiology, location, size, depth, exudates amount, color, and odor; the appearance of wound bed; color: red, yellow, black; and condition of surrounding skin. Braden score of less than 18 or alteration of skin integrity must be evaluated by an RN and document picture (wound photograph apps, date/time, the location of the wound, and staff signature and place in Electronic Health Record (HER) CHI Franciscan Health (2018).

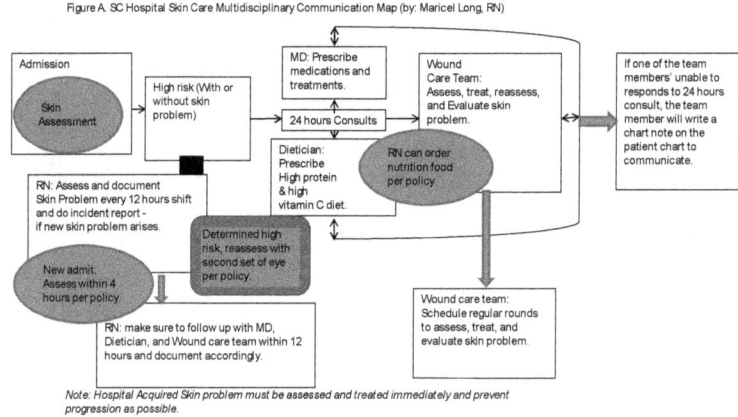

Figure A. SC Hospital Skin Care Multidisciplinary Communication Map (by: Maricel Long, RN)

Note: Hospital Acquired Skin problem must be assessed and treated immediately and prevent progression as possible.

Note: Hospital Acquired Skin problems must be assessed and treated immediately and prevent progression as possible.

SCH is in the Bottom Five

According to the CHI Skin Committee Metrics 2017, SC is in the bottom five on quality and safety outcomes, including the pressure ulcer stages from 1,2,3,4, and unspecified and unstageable (stages 3, 4, and unstageable are included using AHRQ). The policies have been implemented. However, the cause of being in the bottom five of the quality and safety outcomes despite having comprehensive pressure ulcer policies at hand is unknown at this time. My goal is to improve pressure ulcer policies' implementation and improve overall safety and quality outcomes with the use of the Plan-Do-Study- and Act (PDSA) model (Institute for Healthcare Improvement [IHI], 2 018). Overall, SC Hospital's goal is to reduce HAPU as measured on the LOM dashboard and Skin team presentation through policy review and policy implementation as well as policies-driven activities as shown on the Action Plan on pages 23 to 30 of this paper.

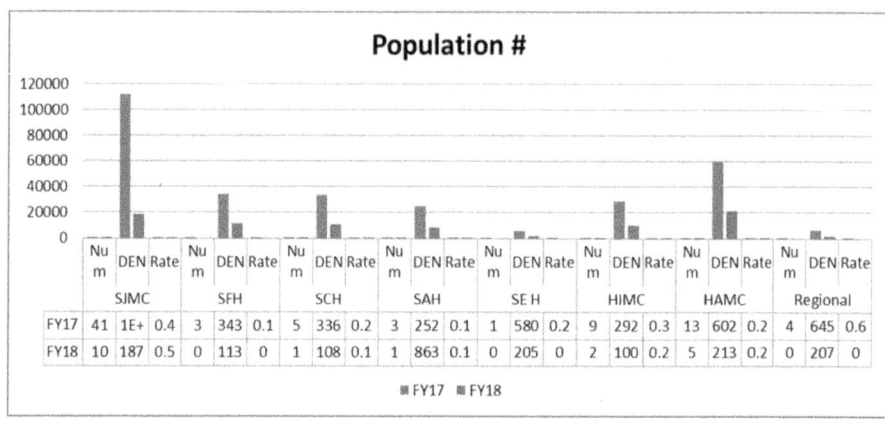

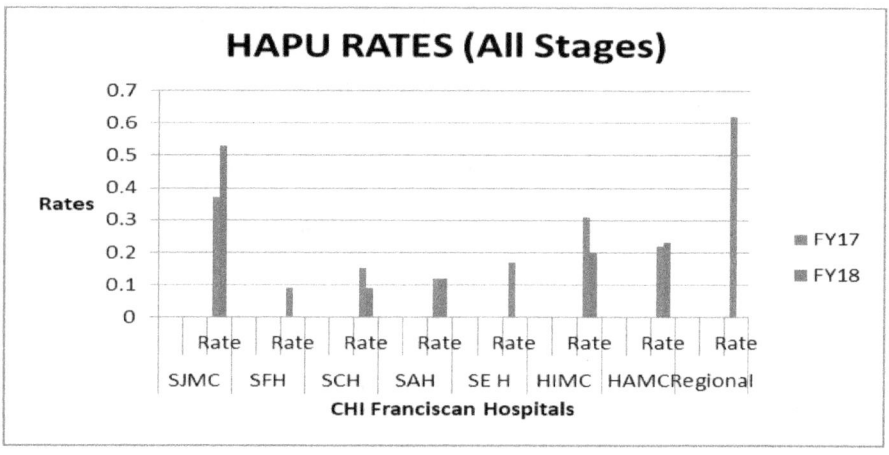

Schreiber (2017)

CHI Franciscan Health Skin Committee Metrics (2017 showed some increase in pressure ulcers in some facilities of CHI Franciscan such as St. Joseph Medical Center and Hyaline Medical Center.

SCH Leadership

According to Soban et al. (2017), Nurse Leaders' roles and influences are necessary for the implementation of a pressure ulcer prevention program so that it will be operationalized at an optimum level. Nurses' leaders and nurses in frontlines of care are necessary for preventing harm to patients and improving patient outcomes (ANA, 2017; and Sherwood & Barnsteiner, 2017). High-quality care is everyone's responsibility, from clinicians to patients; however, quality and safety in healthcare rely on effective nursing strategies (Soban, Kim, Yuan, & Miltner, 2017; Sherwood & Barnsteiner, 2017; ANA, 2017; Reddy et al., 2006; Zrelak et al., 2013).

Soban et al. (2017) included the use of risk assessment tools, strategies to prevent pressure ulcers, policy, committee, staff education, and wound care specialists, as well as the use of performance or performance monitoring incorporated into routine care. However, there were many variations and a lack of consistency in the performance of individualized hospitals, and they were not operationalized consistently. Reddy et al. (2006), suggested the use of support surfaces, mattress overlays on operating tables, specialized foam, and specialized sheepskin overlays as well as every 2 hours turn as appropriate strategies to prevent a pressure ulcer. Reddy et al. (2006) focused on mobility, nutrition, and skin health to prevent a pressure ulcer.

Loudet et al. (2017) utilized multifaceted interventions to manage pressure ulcers, such as the implementation of a multidisciplinary team, educational session for staff, pressure ulcer checklist, smartphone application for lesion monitoring and decision-making, and a family prevention bundle or family participation with open visitation policy shown significant reduction of pressure ulcer. Loudet et al. (2017) also made use of the PDSA model to respond to the question, "What can we improve? Soban et al., 2017 described the presence and operationalization of organizational strategies to support the implementation of pressure ulcer prevention programs across acute care hospitals. These are essentials in the planning and intervention phase and in creating individualized treatment plans for the patient.

At the beginning of spring 2018, the SCH Skin Team created a Skin Team Charter, also known as a site-based skin team. Members of this team are the skin champions from each of the inpatient units: med tele, orthopedic, and critical care. SC champions will serve as the resource for the SCH team to reduce Hospital Acquired Pressure Ulcer (HAP); RN/ charge nurses and CNAs from the day shift and night shift get together with the RN chairperson, quality manager (the main leader of the skin team), the health educator, and all inpatient units' managers in support with this team. This team will assist in decreasing SCH HAPU and help to formulate strategies for improvements. The **Vision:** to reduce HAPU as measured on the Living Our Mission (LOM) dashboard and Skin team presentation. The **Ultimate goal:** to decrease HAPU on the LOM dashboard. Finally, the **Hypothesis:** capturing stage 1&2 PU during admission can decrease HAPU and, therefore, increase reimbursement.

Outcomes measurement

A. Performance Measurement Living Our Mission (LOM) dashboard

- Reduce HAPU as measured on the LOM dashboard and Skin team presentation.

B. Clinical audit

- Nutrition foods – Registered Nurses can order this per policy.

- IRIS – everyone can file this but the communication flow is unclear - to find out if IRIS has been done or has not for an incidence of skin alteration.

- Clarified types of wound cream/lotion: Blue for buttocks and orange for an open wound.

- Clarified types of bed mattresses related to HAPU prevention intervention.

- Clarified Charge Nurses RNs need to take responsibility for calling MD if a wound ostomy nurse is not available in order to obtain an order to initiate pressure injury interventions.

- The Braden score is not being effectively used to drive nursing care.

- Positive reinforcement and just in time training in a non-punitive way.

C. The Regional Skin Conferences

- During this regional skin team meeting held on April 19, 2018, there were several important points noted:

1. Communication between departments to whom the patients were transferred in regards to positioning. Suppose the patient is from the pre-operative room, intra-operative, and post-operative. In that case, the OR nurse, PACU nurse, and in-patient-nurse need to communicate with each other to coordinate patient positioning and wound or any skin alterations.

2. Pressure injuries that happened within 72 hours after surgery could be related to the surgery.

3. Several tools being used to prevent or reduce HAPU are still need validations – they need to be consistent, relevant, and reliable.

4. Positioning diagram to help aid in repositioning the patient.

5. Daily care floLargest Psychiatric Hospitaleet should be utilized as it shows what positioning the patient while in the OR.

6. Since there is a global shortage of wound ostomy nurses, the Charge Nurses RNs on the floor need to take responsibility for calling the MD if a wound ostomy nurse is not available in order to obtain an order to initiate interventions instead of waiting.

7. One representative raised concerns about HAPU cases – Miscounted.

Data Aggregations and Analyses

1. The Trends and Opportunities (November 2017 to May 2018).

- The first data aggregation was from November 2017 to February 2018.

- The results showed:

1. An incongruent assessment was noted: The majority of ICU patients appeared to be a "No Risk," as the majority of the patients appeared to have Braden scores of 19 above.

2. Several forms were not filled out properly: There were 5 forms in PCU and 3 forms in ICU that have no Braden scores.

3. There were wounds or skin problems that were not photographed.

- The quality manager and MN student discussed the data findings.

- The quality manager stated there were incorrect assessments and recommended MN students to meet with the critical care unit (CCU) manager.

- The CCU manager and MN student met and discussed the data findings.

- CCU manager recommended including all parts of the audit forms to look for what part of interventions is missing. She asked, "What part of interventions are we missing?"

- CCU manager stated, "Education will be backed to staff for the incorrect assessment."

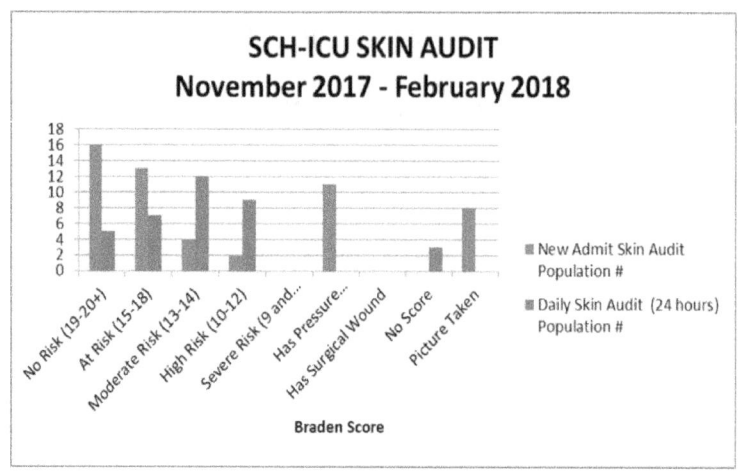

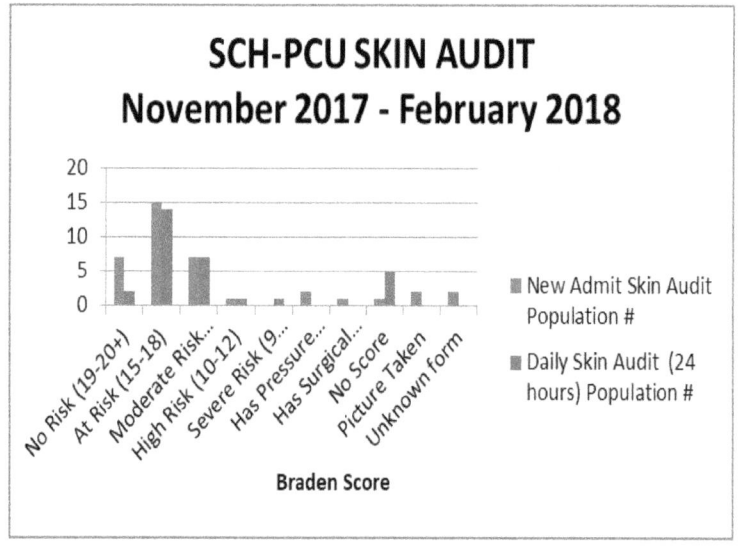

2. The Trends and Opportunities (February to April 2018).

- The second data aggregation was for February to April 2018

- The results showed:

1. All the patients in the ICU have Braden scores of 18 and less, as expected.

2. Upon admission, pressure ulcer stages 3 - 4, and unstageable were captured.

3. The new admit skin audits showed good capturing of stage 1 -2 pressure ulcers (Capturing stage 1 -2 pressure ulcers is an indication of good assessment to prevent HAPU).

4. The majority of the patients were provided correct surfaces; however:

   o In the ICU, there were three out of five that were not on the correct surfaces.

o   In the PCU, there were seven out of 64 patients were

not on the correct surfaces.

No pressure ulcer was noted on the 24 hours daily audits.

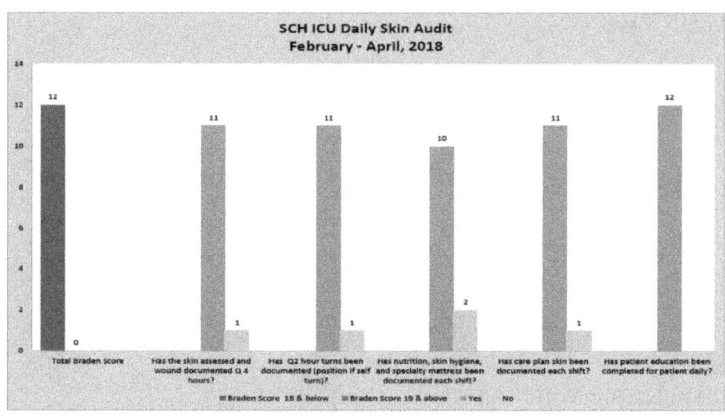

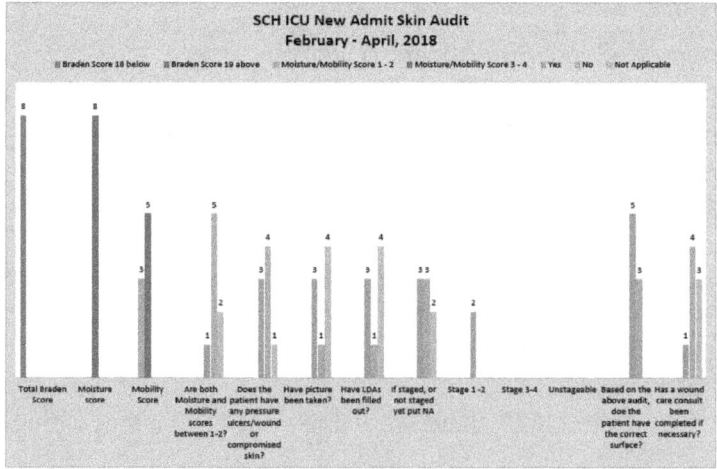

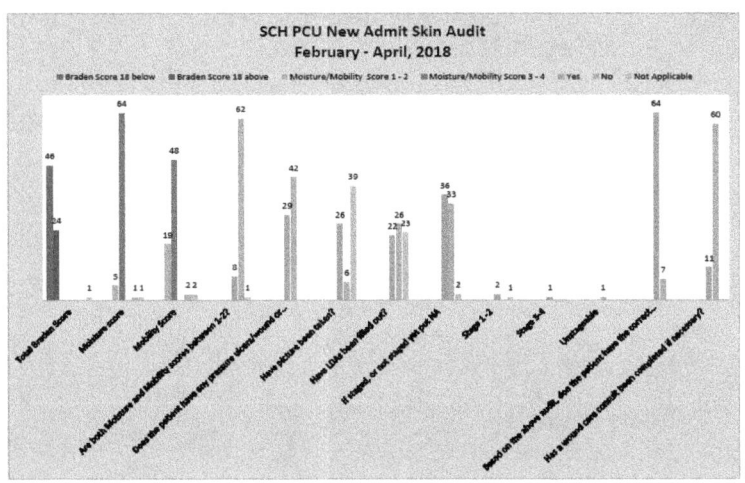

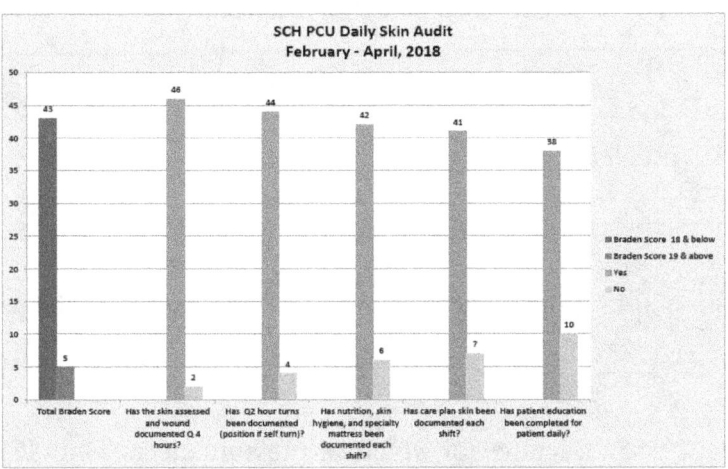

3. The Trends and Opportunities (April to May 2018).

- The third data aggregation was for April to May 2018.

- The results showed:

1. All ICU and PCU patients appeared to have Braden scores below 18.

2. Plan skin documentation for each shift:

o ICU daily audit showed 2 out of 11 patients have no care plan skin documentation each shift.

3. PCU appeared that LDAs were not utilized in all skin problems;

o One LDA was not filled out.

4. Correct surfaces were not utilized for all the patients who are at high risk for PU.

5. Pictures for wound or pressure ulcers: Both ICU and PCU showed 100% photographed.

6. Pressure ulcer stage 2 captured during admission-(good).

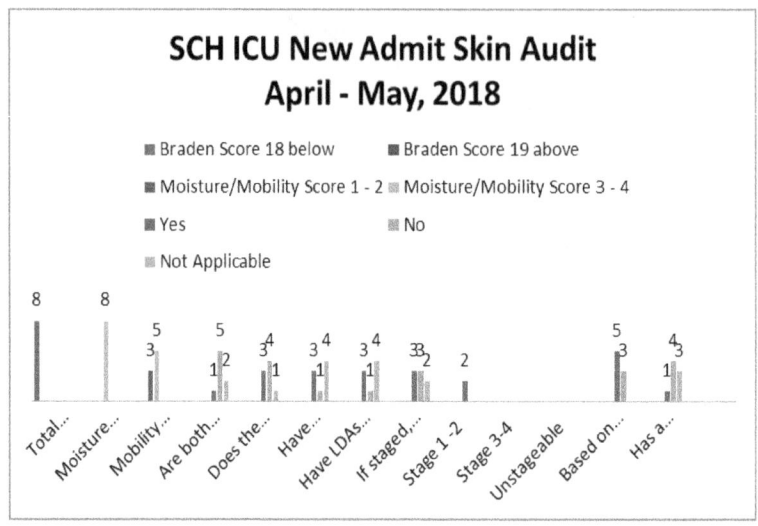

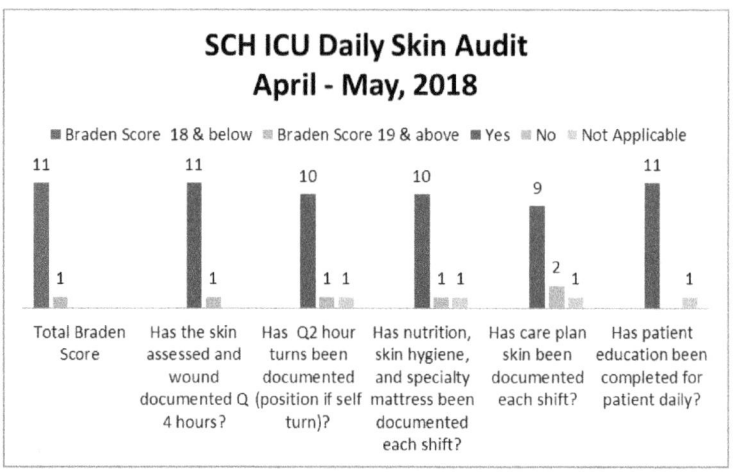

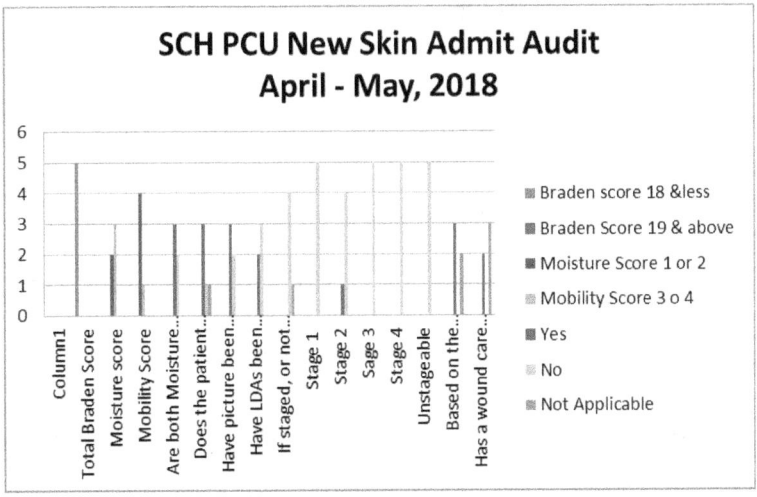

The SCH Action Plan

- **CHI, in general, has a mission to heal and a promise to care.**

- **Values:** Reverence - Profound respect and awe for all creation, the foundation that shapes spirituality, our relationships with others and our journey to God; Integrity - Moral wholeness, soundness, fidelity, trust and truthfulness in all we do; Compassion - Solidarity with one another and the capacity to enter into another's joy and sorrow; Excellence - Achieving preeminent performance, becoming the benchmark and putting forth our personal and professional best

  (https://www.chifranciscan.org/about-us/overview/mission-vision-and-values.html).

- **Strategic Priorities 2017-2019**

The CHI Pacific Northwest Division will focus on quality, safety and exceptional experiences for our patients to position us as the premier health system in the Pacific Northwest. To achieve our priorities, we will:

1. Achieve the 75th percentile for quality, safety and patient experience.

2. Be the best place to work and practice

3. Achieve excellence in operational and financial performance

4. Be one CHI Pacific Northwest

5. Improve the health of defined populations

6. Engage the community to support our mission (https://www.chifranciscan.org/about-us/overview/mission-vision-and-values.html)

In order to track incidence from IRIS, I am proposing this tracking sheet to track daily pressure ulcer incidence. This way, we can avoid redundancy (many staff reported having difficulty or not sure if the IRIS has been done or not done on pressure ulcer incidence.) There is no way to track incidence, which is very concerning to me as a master-level

RN. The IT department has to find ways to improve this communication with the IRIS to the nursing staff specifically RNs. Therefore, this tracking sheet that I created will prevent confusion as to whether the IRIS has been or has not been done. I suggest placing this at the nurses' station (inside the charge nurse's office, attached to the wall). This incidence tracking sheet can also serve as a quality indicator, as we can track how many pressure injuries are observed in a month by just looking at this tracking sheet. The source of this idea is from all the policy reviews and literature reviews, including the poster of Walter, Jamison, Zafer, and Sanders (2016) and overall experience as a nurse.

Tracking Sheet: Daily Pressure Ulcer Incidence per IRIS (By: Maricel Long, RN/ MN student)							
Month/Year: May 2018			Department: ICU				
IRIS #/Pt. #	Stages: 1,2,3,4, & Unstageable/Unspecified	Present on Admission? (√)	HAPU? (√)	Q2 hours turn compliance (yes/no)	Incidence Date: mo/dd/yy	Monthly Total	

The goal in Reducing HAPU: Decrease HAPU on the LOM dashboard.

Objectives:

- By the end of summer 2018, SCH Site Based Skin Team champions will be able to build rapport with each direct care staff in each department: ICU, PCU, Medtele, and Orthopedic.

  o "Open-mindedness of the nursing staff and willingness to try something new."

o   Managers from different departments raise awareness and encourage direct care staff to full cooperation with Site Based Skin team project implementation to reduce HAPU and prevent pressure injuries.

• By the beginning of autumn 2018, nurses and other nursing staff received training on the monitoring system and on patient turning and repositioning techniques for proper offloading, bed types for certain conditions, and nutritional regimen utilized.

o   Teamwork approach for interventions to prevent HAPU.

o   Data tools such as the orchid rounding tool, including the Pressure Ulcer daily IRIS tracking sheet, have been utilized for efficiency and effectiveness.

• By March 2019, data had been aggregated and analyzed.

o   "Sharing daily compliance data with nursing staff as an ongoing quality metric."

- By the end of spring 2019, the reduction of HAPU will be up to 100%, as shown on the LOM dashboard and Skin team presentation.

"Nursing leadership support is crucial for getting staff nurse buy-in" with the implementation of the SCH Site Based Skin team project implementation. Data will need to be collected to show statistical significance in HAPU reduction (Walter, Jamison, Zafer, Sanders (2016).

SCH Action Plan Logic Model			
Resources	**Activities**	**Outputs**	**Outcomes**
SCH quality manager as the main leader of the Site Based Skin team project and regional skin team.	Building rapport to each direct care staffs in each department: ICU, PCU, Medtele, and Orthopedic – encouraging ("Open mindedness of the nursing staff and willingness to try something new").	Developed a sustainable skin based team project with a Mission, Vision, Goal, and SMART Objectives for the project and each activity.	
Managers from different departments: ICU, PCU, Medtele, and Orthopedic	Managers from different departments raise awareness and encourage direct care staffs full cooperation of Site Based Skin team project implementation to reduce HAPU and prevent pressure injuries.	Identified and recruited Site based Skin team champions -all survived 100%.	
SCH health educator.	Health educators supporting the Site Based Skin team by reviewing work and activities as appropriate.	Established bi-monthly x 12 months meetings for SCH Site based Skin team (four hours each meeting).	Reduction of HAPU up to 100% as shown on the LOM dashboard and Skin team presentation.
SCH site based skin team champions: RNs and CNAs.	Nurses and other nursing staffs receiving training on the monitoring system and on patient turning and repositioning technique for proper offloading, bed types for certain condition and nutritional regimens (establishing teamwork approach for interventions to prevent HAPU).	All managers or department leaders have established rapport and awareness about the Site based Skin project implementation.	
Regional Skin team conferences	Data tool such as orchid rounding tool including the Pressure Ulcer daily IRIS tracking sheet (proposed by UWT MN student for efficiency and effectiveness).	Identified SCH IT room as conference rooms for all meetings, seminars or even just in time couching sessions.	
University of Washington, Tacoma (UWT) Master of nursing student and volunteer.	Data Aggregation and analysis ("Sharing daily compliance data with nursing staffs as an ongoing quality metric").	Accomplished quarterly data aggregation and analysis by UWT MN student or volunteer.	

Space: Conference rooms in schools	Continues bi-monthly site skin based skin team meeting and communication with the regional skin team.		
Equipment: pens, notebook, tape recorders	Meetings, seminars, and conferences – presentation with regional skin team (Power point presentation on minutes while keeping track on the progress).		
Educational Materials: PowerPoint presentations, handouts, flyers, checklists.	Just in time discussion, coaching, and practice with direct care staffs		
Funding: SCH fund (Franciscan Health System Organization).	➢ Quarterly data aggregation and analysis (utilize UWT MN student or volunteer). ➢ Collect and analyze data for further evaluation.		

Leadership Challenge

Decision-makers cannot hope to develop and implement new strategies for quality without properly engaging healthcare providers, communities, and service users. Healthcare providers need to operate within an appropriate policy environment for quality and with a proper understanding of the needs and expectations of those they serve in order to deliver the best results. Moreover, communities and service users need to influence both quality policy and the way in which health services are provided to them if they are to improve their own health outcomes (Castner, Foltz-Ramos, Schwartz, & Ceravolo, 2012; Gittell, Hoffer, Beswick, Goldmann, & Wallack, 2015; and Sherwood & Barnsteiner, 2012)

As a leader in healthcare delivery, I must support improving teamwork and collaboration between inter-professionals in healthcare delivery. Effective team leaders organize the team, identify and articulate clear goals and each member's responsibilities, communicate changes and follow-ups, and encourage team members to collaborate. Effective team members enable conflict resolution in a learning environment, and model effective teamwork—a teamwork that offers a powerful solution to improving collaboration and communication. Effective communication is a necessary skill to build an effective and efficient team, which is essential in preventing and alleviating errors that cause injury and harm to the patient. The result is high-quality healthcare outcomes (Castner, Foltz-Ramos, Schwartz, & Ceravolo, 2012; Gittell, Hoffer, Beswick, Goldmann, & Wallack, 2015; and Sherwood & Barnsteiner, 2012).

PDSA Cycle

Plan (P) –
➤ Reduce Hospital Acquired Pressure Ulcer (HAPU) at SC Hospital as measured on the Living Our Mission (LOM) dashboard and Skin team presentation.
➤ Cost-effectiveness after all interventions.
Do (D) –
➤ Recommendations:
o Apply multifaceted leadership strategies in order to assess compliance.
o Collect data and synthesize data to find gaps/trends
o Ensure utilization of existing policies which are founded in evidence - based practice.
o The nurse leaders' roles and influences are necessary for the implementation of pressure ulcer prevention intervention so that it will be operationalized at an optimum level (Soban, Kim, Yuan, & Miltner, 2017).
o Proper assessment and documentation are essential to ensure safety and quality nursing care outcomes (Zrelak, Utter, Sadeghi, Cuny, Baron, & Romano, 2013).
o Continue consistency for all HAPU prevention interventions: The risk assessment tools, strategies to prevent pressure ulcers, policy, committee, staff education, wound care specialists, and the use of performance or performance monitoring incorporated into routine care.
o Improve the communication between risk management personnel and quality management personnel.
o Information Technology (IT) to create a clear way to communicate IRIS so that the floor staff, RNs and CNAs will have a clear view of IRIS and also to avoid redundancy.

o The tools being used to prevent or reduce HAPU need to be validated.

o Utilize the positioning diagram to help aid in repositioning the patient – this needs to be utilized optimally.

o Utilize daily care floLargest Psychiatric Hospitaleet should be utilized as it shows what positioning the patient while in the OR.

o The Charge Nurses and RNs on the floor need to take responsibility for calling the MD as soon as a pressure ulcer is observed if a wound ostomy nurse is not available in order to obtain an order to initiate interventions immediately.

Study (S) –

• Data analysis and review the findings with the data collected and create a plan to solve the problem.

• Review the interventions provided and discuss what went well, what went poorly, and what could be improved for the next time.

• Discuss what you have learned.

Act (A) –

• Proceed with the new learning by applying what has been learned (do better at this time). Continue the routine.

• Structure: Doctors, Nurses/nursing staff, Housekeeping, Patients and the patient's family.

• Process: PCU protocol and guidelines, Skin Care Policy and Assessment Policy.

• Outcome: Reduction of PCU Hospital Acquired Pressure Ulcer and cost-effectiveness.

Learning Derived

I am very impressed that SC Hospital people are just like families and friends at work; they are united and striving for the quality of their jobs. I have met and spoken to the frontline staff RNs and CNAs. I have spoken to the operating room staff while I was at the cafeteria, the floor staff, the cafeteria and store staff, and most of all, the volunteers—where I came from and where I started my career as a nurse. Nonetheless, during this spring quarter of 2018, I have met most of the SC Hospital leadership team: I met the director of nursing, the assistant director, the managers from the different departments, and the manager from acute care, med tele, and orthopedic. I also met their health educator. I am seeing their support, even just through a simple hi, smile, and bye. I appreciate everything that they are doing in reference to hard work because they are striving to reduce HAPU for quality and safety.

References

ANA (2017). Nursing quality. Retrieved from: http://www.nursingworld.org/ncn (Links to an external site.)Links to an external site.g

American Nurses Association (ANA) (2017). Nursing quality. Retrieved from: http://www.nursingworld.org/ncn (Links to an external site.)Links to an external site.g

American Association of Colleges of Nursing's (AACN) (2018). Essentials of Master's Education in Nursing. Retrieved from: http://www.aacn.nche.edu/education-resources/essential-series

Agency for Health care Research and Quality [AHRQ] (2016). AHRQ quality indicators. Retrieved from: http://www.qualityindicators.ahrq.gov/Default.aspx

Castner, J., Foltz-Ramos, K., Schwartz, D., & Ceravolo, D. (2012). A leadership challenge: Staff nurse perceptions after an organizational TeamSTEPPS initiative. The Journal of Nursing Administration, 42(10), 467-72.

Gittell, Hoffer, Beswick, Goldmann, & Wallack,(2015). Teamwork methods for accountable care: Relational coordination and TeamSTEPPS. Health Care Management Review, 40(2), 116-25.

CHI Franciscan Health (2018). Mission, Vision and Values. Retrieved from: https://www.chifranciscan.org/about-us/overview/mission-vision-and-values.html

CHI Franciscan Health (2018). Assessment: Patient admission assessment and reassessment policy, 951.25 (Policy Stat ID: 1803033)

CHI Franciscan Health (2018). Skin care and pressure ulcer prevention policy (adult inpatient) 961.00 (Policy Stat ID: 3854690)

Institute of Healthcare Improvement [IHI](2018).Tool. Retrieved.http://www.ihi.org/resources/Pages/Tools/PlanDoStudyActWorksheet.aspx

Loudet, C., Marchena, M., Maradeo, M., Fernández, S., Romero, M., Valenzuela, G., Estenssoro, E. (2017). Reducing pressure ulcers in patients with prolonged acute mechanical ventilation: A quasi-experimental study. Revista Brasileira De Terapia Intensiva, 29(1), 39-46.

Ostomy wound management (OWM) (2018).Skin Matters: Impaired Skin Integrity in the Elderly. Retrieved from: http://www.o-wm.com/content/impaired-skin-integrity-elderly

Reddy, M., Gill, S., Rochon, P. (2006). Preventing pressure ulcers: A systematic review. JAMA. 2006; 296(8):974–984. doi:10.1001/jama.296.8.974

Schreiber, A. (2017). *Skin committee metric.* [data file].

Sherwood, G., & Barnsteiner, J. (2012). Quality and Safety in nursing: A competency approach to improving outcomes (2nd ed.). Chichester, UK: Wiley-Blackwell

Soban, L., Kim, L., Yuan, A., & Miltner, R. (2017). Organisational strategies to implement hospital pressure ulcer prevention programs: Findings from a national survey. *Journal of Nursing Management, 25*(6), 457-467.

The W. Edward Deming Institute (2018). Deming 101: Theory of knowledge and the PDSA improvement and learning cycle. Retrieved from: https://blog.deming.org/2013/12/deming-101-theory-of-knowledge-and-the-pdsa-improvement-and-learning-cycle/

Walter B., Jamison K., Zafer D., Sanders T., (2016). Transforming pressure ulcer prevention in the ICU with patient wearable technology and nursing leadership. JPS Texas Organization Nurse Executive Poster.

Zrelak, P., Utter, G., Sadeghi, B., Cuny, J., Baron, R., & Romano, P. (2013). Using the Agency for Healthcare Research and Quality patient safety indicators for targeting nursing quality improvement. *The Journal of Nursing Administration, 43*(10 Suppl), S51-60.

Community Health Need Assessment

By

D. Brogan,

M. Long,

Z. Woldselassie

2017

This paper is a continuance of "Community Health Assessment and Planning Analysis Paper Part I," submitted for this course on May 18, 2017. This paper will describe 3 ideas for improving the Community Health Needs Assessment (CHNA) completed by CHI Franciscan, SC Hospital in Lakewood, Washington. We will discuss the leadership steps we propose to implement change in the identified community of interest. This proposal will justify alignment with the identified strategies from the CHNA published by SC Hospital. The purpose is to be able to do a Community Health Nursing Assessment of youth smokers of Pierce County's residents aged 18 and below. Counting, assessing, and examining youth smokers of Pierce County's residents aged 18 and below needs. What is currently being done to resolve identified needs? How well have the identified needs been addressed in the past? Identify the most significant health problem within a population of youth smokers of Pierce County's residents aged 18 and below. What is SC Hospital's capacity to address specific health problems, interventions related to identified health problems, and strengths, resources, and assets within the community? Formulate strategies to solve the problem of what Clover Park School District does for youth smokers. The purpose of this paper is to describe a least 3 ideas for improving this assessment based on the class readings. Develop leadership steps you would take, including identifying who will be on your committee, describing your purpose (describe 1) and objectives (describe at least 3), and determining what assessment tools you would plan to use based on limited resource allocation for assessment and planning. Develop a basic list of questions that you could use with these tools. Identify community stakeholders who should participate, including educators, government officials, law enforcement officials, hospital administrators, social workers, leaders of civic organizations, and students.

OBJECTIVE

Vision: Our Vision: Lakewood-A community free of the death and disease caused by tobacco.

Mission: Our Mission is to develop and implement smoking prevention and cessation programs focusing on the youth serviced by SC Hospital.

Objectives:

Reduce tobacco usage by 10% every year for the next 5 years through community intervention. Within 5 years, 50% of current smokers will have quit smoking. 100% of those who have never smoked continue to identify themselves as non-smokers.

Evaluate the youth tobacco use of the city of Lakewood residents aged 18 and below. Provide instructions to students who volunteer to do a survey at the City of Lakewood with the use of questionnaires or flyers. Provide pre and post-survey.

Tools

Windshields Survey:

Observe for apparent teen smokers. Observe for tobacco advertisements (map) (Indian reservation/tobacco shops/small stores/billboards)

Surveys: 10-12 questions, Paper, Email, outside stores, Parks. Community meetings (4: 2 days & 2 eves).

The Law

WA State RCW 26.28.080, Minors cannot buy cigarettes. It is illegal for anyone, including parents, to sell or give cigarettes to youth. Indoor clean air laws (25 ft from doors) Parks are becoming smoke-free zones. Additional States: less restrictive for tobacco use. (For Example: Kentucky)

Identify Committee: City of Lakewood

Lakewood Police Dept. (Chief Mike Zaro, CSOs-Community Service Officers, ask for interested parties); Lakewood Juvenile Court System; Parks and Recreation

Mary Dodsworth Director of; Parks, Recreation and Community Services (Lakewood Community Center). Mayor: Don Anderson (Deputy Mayor-Jason Whalen or city council representative). South Sound Military and Communities Partnership: Bill Adamson Program Manager. Community Members: Pierce County Health Department, UWT Student (Class or Specific), Local Radio Station (Support), Local Newspaper (Support), Clover Park School District, Superintendent Office (Debbie LeBeau-Superintendent), Board of Directors: Marty Schafer, Becki Kellcy, Carole Jacobs, Joe Vlaming, Paul Wagemann, Director of Community Relations: Kim Prentice, Clover Park Parent-Teacher Organization. Schools: 16 Elementary Schools, 5 Middle Schools, 3 High Schools. That is not in school: Homeless, Incarcerated, by choice. Youth: Where are they?

Partnerships: For success. Interventions: Flyers, Incentives, Education.

BACKGROUND

Lakewood is a city in Pierce County, Washington, United States. The population was 58,163 at the 2010 census. Lakewood was officially incorporated on February 28, 1996. Historical names include Tacoma/Lakewood Center and Lakes District. Lakewood is the second-largest city in Pierce County and is home to the Clover Park School District.

SC Hospital utilized data collected from multiple resources identifying the healthcare needs of the population serviced by their facility.

As stated in Part I of this paper, a paper survey received 712 responses. Understanding who lives in a community is the first step toward understanding that community's health needs. The demographic characteristics of a community are strong predictors of health outcomes and health service needs. For example, communities with large older populations may have different health needs than a younger population. Factors such as lower income and education levels are also strongly linked to worse health outcomes. Population – Approximately 308,248 people live in the CHI Franciscan Health SC Hospital primary service area: an increase of 54,582 residents or a 21.5% growth since 1990. Age – Children, teens, and youth represent 35.0% of the population, while 12.5% of the population is 65 or older. Respectively, these numbers are 32.2% and 14.0% statewide, not significantly different. Race and Ethnicity – A little over one-half of residents are White non-Hispanic (56.0%). Hispanic residents were the second largest group, representing 13.5% of the service area's total population; statewide, they account for 12.2%.

PROCESS

Establish survey sites such as Safeway and Albertson, and in front of the Clover Park School District store. Funding and partnership with key stakeholders. Gather survey volunteers. Designated UWT MN students to collaborate with volunteers and stakeholders. UWT MN students to provide education to volunteers for pre and post survey of youth tobacco used. UWT will collaborate with stakeholders and volunteer students to provide education to residents and families about youth Tobacco use and provide education to residents aged 18 and below every 6 months. Pre-post survey every 6 months for the next 5 years. Improvement of ongoing intervention.

CONCLUSION AND RECOMMENDATIONS

The UWT MN students will collaborate with the designated volunteers, stakeholders, and SC Hospital representatives to obtain data on youth tobacco use in the City of Lakewood. The Volunteers will survey the designated areas in the City of Lakewood: Safeway, Albertson, and Clover Park School District every 6 months to assess improvements and follow-ups needed. The Residents of Lakewood will be educated about Youth Tobacco used bi-annually and encourage more residents' participation at each meeting. Collaboration with Stakeholders, Lakewood leadership, SC Hospital, and Clover Park School District will reduce tobacco usage by 10% every year for the next 5 years through community intervention. 50% of current smokers will have quit smoking, and 100% of those who have never smoked continue to identify themselves as non-smokers. Collaboration or partnership will help to improve the health of the youth residents in Lakewood.

Precede Model:

Phase 1: Social Assessment: In 2011, 12.3 percent of the Pierce County population was living below the poverty level, compared to Washington State, which had a 13.9 percent population and the nation with a 15.9 percent population living below the poverty level. For children under the age of 18, 15.7 percent were living below the poverty level, compared to the state's poverty level of 18.3 percent and the nation's 22.5 percent. Lower educational attainment and low income are associated with poorer health and tobacco use. Healthcare inequalities, as well as inequitable access to education and inadequate job skills and training, were identified as major problems in Pierce County (Peirce County Community Health Status Assessment, 2013)

According to the report, in Washington State, there are about 40 young people who start smoking every day. As CHNA's report stated, cigarette smoking is the leading cause of preventable disease and death in the United States. From the same report, in 2014, the CHI Franciscan Health St Clare Hospital service area's 10th graders have a smoking rate of 10.4%, compared to that of Washington state's, which is 8.0%. A more significant portion is from white youth as opposed to non-white youth. One of the factors that cause poor health outcomes is health behaviors (30%), which are a close second to socioeconomic factors (40%) in this service area. Based on the CHNA report, CHI Franciscan Health SC Hospital's priority health concern is tobacco use among adults and youth (CHI Franciscan Health SC Hospital Community Health Needs Assessment, 2016; TPCHD, 2016).

Community members also voiced the need for tobacco prevention and cessation services as smoking continues to plague residents. The rate of smoking is above the state rate and the Healthy People 2020 national objective. Residents also identified poverty-related issues such as hunger, lack of transportation, unemployment, homelessness, and affordable housing as barriers to health care. Non-white residents of Pierce County were disproportionately impacted compared to white residents. Health disparities came up at community workshops and in the Pierce County Community Survey in the context of people's inability to access quality health services and health insurance. Pierce County participants provided feedback about residents facing racial disparities, language barriers, unemployment, and poverty and how these issues cause barriers to accessing health care. Lack of access to health care was identified as an issue having the greatest impact on health. Residents frequently mentioned barriers to accessing care and the impacts of not having access to quality health care. Social determinants of health and the devastating health inequity currently plaguing the nation will not be solved quickly or by any one profession or organization. The vast and complex structural changes required at every level of society will require the participation of the nation as a whole. Nurses can lead other healthcare professionals in a national educational campaign surrounding the impact of societal determinants of health. Nurses can also help leaders outside of the health care system understand the ways in which their decisions can impact the health of U.S. residents. Finally, policymakers need to be educated about the role of social determinants of health on the health status and future of the nation (Braveman et al., 2011; CHI Franciscan Health SC Hospital Community Health Needs Assessment, 2016; Lathrop, B. 2013; TPCHD, 2016; and McKenzie et al., 2013).

Phase 2: Epidemiological assessment:

LEADING CAUSES OF DEATH

Over the last five years, the main causes of death in the US have remained fairly consistent, with the top three of these (heart disease, cancer and chronic lower respiratory diseases) accounting for over 50% of all deaths. The top three leading causes of death in the CHI Franciscan Health SC Hospital service area from 2010 to 2014 were heart disease, cancers of all types and lung cancer. The top ten leading causes of death were the same for the residents of the hospital service area as they were for all Washington state residents.

LEADING CAUSES OF HOSPITALIZATION

Another aspect of the health of a community is the rate of hospitalizations. When compared to other states, Washington State's rate of hospitalizations for conditions that can be prevented by early intervention or good outpatient care was lower than the average in 2011. From 2010 to 2014, hospitalizations for childbirth accounted for the majority of the hospitalizations in the CHI Franciscan Health SC Hospital service area, followed by circulatory and digestive disorders. The leading causes of hospitalization and their ranking were identical for the hospital service area and the state. Leading causes of hospitalization by the main category of diagnosis, 2010-2014 average.

Cigarette smoking is the leading cause of preventable disease and death in the United States. The Centers for Disease Control and Prevention estimate that cigarette smoking kills about 8,300 adults each year in Washington state. From 2011 to 2013, the CHI Franciscan Health SC Hospital service area had a higher percent (23.5%) of current smokers than did Washington State (16.8%). Cigarette smoking rates ranged from 1.8% to 44.0% for specific zip codes in the CHI Franciscan Health SC Hospital service area (Figure 5).

Most adult smokers begin smoking as teenagers. In Washington State, about 40 youths start smoking cigarettes each day, and one in three of these youth smokers will die prematurely from a smoking-caused disease. Additionally, smoking is associated with an increased risk of drug use and low academic performance. In 2014, 10.3% of 10th graders in the CHI Franciscan Health SC Hospital service area smoked. This rate was slightly higher than Washington

State's rate (8.0%). A significantly higher percentage of Whites smoked (12.6%) than did non-Whites (8.2%).

Findings from the 2014 National Youth Tobacco Survey, as well as the statewide Healthy Youth Survey, show that e-cigarette use among high school students has increased three-fold in just the two previous years. In the CHI Franciscan Health SC Hospital service area, the percentage of 10th graders who used an e-cigarette in the past 30 days was 22.4%. *

LIFE EXPECTANCY

Life expectancy is a widely used measure of the overall health of a population. The definition is the average number of years a person at birth can expect to live, given current death rates. Life expectancy can be improved by reducing specific causes of diseases and eliminating health inequities. For the CHI Franciscan Health SC service area, the average life expectancy of a resident for those born in the years 2010 to 2014 is 78 years, two years lower than the state average of 80 years. Statewide, residents are living longer. The average life expectancy for those born in the years 2010 to 2014 is about five years longer than for those born in 1980. Patterns in life expectancy data by race in the service area indicate that American Indian/Alaska Native and Native Hawaiian/Other Pacific Islanders had the shortest life expectancies: 73 and 71 years, respectively. Hispanics and Asians had the longest life expectancies, at 86 and 84 years, respectively.

Life expectancy in the CHI Franciscan Health SC Hospital service areas varied by geography, ranging from 70.7 to 81.8 years of age (Figure 4). The lowest life expectancies are in the Tacoma, Parkland/Spanaway and Spring Brook communities.

Assets and Resources:

CHI Franciscan Health Outpatient Nutrition Education Center; CHI Franciscan Health Diabetes Support Groups-St. Joseph Medical Center and St. Anthony Hospital; CHI Institute for Research & Innovation; CHI Franciscan Health Talks; Local parks and community centers offer public places for physical activities; some offer programs such as single-gender swim times and scholarships for children; Supplemental and Nutrition Assistance Program (SNAP-Ed) The goal of SNAP-Ed is to improve the likelihood that persons eligible for SNAP will make healthy choices within a limited budget and choose active lifestyles consistent with the current Dietary Guidelines for Americans and My Plate; Farmers markets; The Women Infant and Children Supplemental Nutrition Program helps pregnant women, new mothers, and young children eat well, learn about nutrition, and stay healthy; Food banks and other feeding programs, sponsored by faith-based organizations, are working to provide healthier options to their customers; Ready Set Go! 5210 is a community-based initiative in Pierce County to promote healthy lifestyle choices for children, youth and families; YMCA Programs: Diabetes Prevention Program; Silver Sneakers; ACT Program Opportunities include providing information about free or low-cost cooking and exercise programs in languages read by immigrants and refugees. Provide healthy ethnic cooking classes for minority communities. Improving access to places for physical activity supported by ongoing efforts of employers, coalitions, agencies, and communities. These groups are attempting to change the local environment (e.g., by creating walking trails), build new exercise facilities, provide access to existing nearby facilities, and reduce the cost of opportunities for physical activity. Improved access is typically achieved in a particular community through a multi-component strategy that includes training or education for participants.

Phase 3: Educational & ecological assessment

High school graduation rates: Graduation rates are important indicators of the health status of students in kindergarten through 12th grade. The four-year graduation rate for students in the CHI Franciscan Health SC Hospital service area for the 2013-14 school year was 79.1%. This is higher than Washington State's rate of 77.2%.

About one-third (32.4%) of CHI Franciscan Health SC Hospital service area students in public kindergarten through 12th-grade schools during the 2013-14 school year received free or reduced-price meals. This is significantly higher than the Washington state average of 46.0%.

Phase 4: Administrative & Policy Assessment and Intervention Alignment.

The Affordable Care Act (ACA, 2010) requires that once every three years nonprofit hospitals conduct a CHNA. This report is a collection of data on more than sixty health indicators that represent the health behaviors, outcomes and status of residents of the CHI Franciscan Health SC Hospital service area in Pierce County. In addition, this report includes community input from Pierce County residents gathered at nine community workshops, seven key informant interviews and a survey of more than 700 community residents and partners. CHI Franciscan Health SC Hospital is in Lakewood, Washington. For purposes of this assessment, the CHI Franciscan Health SC Hospital service area includes all residents in a geographic area defined by 13 zip codes surrounding the hospital.

This CHNA will help guide CHI Franciscan Health SC Hospital in providing high-quality, affordable health care for the members of the community that it serves. Moving forward with a community benefit implementation strategy based on the results of this report will assist in making long-term, sustainable changes and strengthening relationships with other partners working to improve community health.

This report was completed in accordance with the Affordable Care Act and includes a description of the community served, leading causes of death, levels of chronic illness and other important community health issues and needs.

Listed below are eight broad categories of community health needs identified for the CHI Franciscan Health SC Hospital service area.

1) Life Expectancy and Leading Causes of Death

2) Chronic Illnesses

3) Actual Causes of Illnesses

4) Access to Care, Uses of Clinical Preventative Services and Oral Health

5) Maternal and Child Health

6) Preventable Causes of Death

7) Violence and Injury Prevention

8) Behavioral Health

The population and environment of a hospital service area may influence the nature of health outcomes. Similarly, relationships between health indicators can affect the degree and/or type of outcome. For instance, a service area with a high rate of tobacco use among its residents may result in a decrease in life expectancy due to the risk of developing cancer. A low birth weight may affect an infant's life expectancy due to the risk of health complications developing later in life. The accessibility and quality of health care for those living in poverty also influence health outcomes, potentially affecting their life expectancy.

This CHNA was completed through a multi-stage process designed to integrate findings from secondary data with the experiences, expertise and opinions made available through primary data collection. Input was gathered from community residents and community stakeholders representing the broad interests of the communities served by hospitals and health systems. Interviews with community residents, organizations and coalitions and an online survey were used to glean feedback and recommendations. Survey and interview questions, along with methodologies, are further described in the Supplement section at the end of this report.

Approximately 60 indicators were chosen that, when looked at together, help illustrate the health of the community. Demographic data and data on key socioeconomic drivers of health status—including poverty, housing and educational attainment—are provided first. This is followed by the data and analysis of each health indicator and main themes identified through the community engagement methods.

When hospital service area data was not available, Pierce County data was used. Washington state data served as the point of reference and comparison. Data limitations and information gaps. This CHNA presents a robust set of secondary data indicators that enable a broad view of the health needs of the CHI Franciscan Health SC Hospital service area. However, as in all data reports, there are some limitations to these findings: Some data for a hospital service area are unavailable, making an assessment at this regional level challenging. Disaggregated data regarding age, race, ethnicity, and gender are not available for all of the data indicators, which limits the ability to look at disparities of health inequities in the community. Data for the CHI Franciscan Health SC Hospital service area may be limited by the size of the population, requiring the averaging of several years of data. This limits the ability of the report to represent the most current state of health. Data is not always collected on an annual basis, resulting in the use of data that is several years old.

While efforts were made to distribute the survey to people of all genders, races/ethnicities and ages, survey participants were disproportionately female and middle-aged (45-59 years). The three most common zip codes of survey participants were 98405, 98406 and 98407, each representing 7.0% of all respondents.

SOCIOECONOMIC CHARACTERISTICS

Poverty: Seventeen percent of residents had incomes below the federal poverty level. One of every three Hispanic residents and residents of "some other race" lives below the Federal Poverty Level. One of every five Black residents, American Indian/Alaska Native residents and residents of two or more races lives below the Federal Poverty Level. Thirty-eight percent of residents live in or below 200% of the federal poverty level, a common eligibility criterion for assistance programs. The rate of poverty varied in the CHI Franciscan Health SC Hospital service area from between 7.4% and 26.3% (Figure 3).

Housing Affordability: More than half of renters (55.2%) and 42.2% of owners with a mortgage in the service area are paying more than 30% of their household income on housing. Spending more than 30% of household income on housing is financially burdensome.

Immigration: Fourteen percent of the service area population is foreign-born. Among people who do not exclusively speak English at home, about nine percent speak English "less than very well."

Homeless

Homelessness is an increasing problem due in part to poverty and inequities in housing. Depending on the size of the service area, the percentage of total homeless people served can vary widely. The Homelessness Housing and Assistance requires each county in the state to conduct an annual Point in Time count of sheltered and unsheltered homeless persons. The most recent Point in Time counts took place on January 29, 2015. The Pierce County count totaled 2,048 homeless, while the Washington state total was 6,893. Of the homeless counted in the CHI Franciscan Health SC Hospital service area, the percentage ranged from a high of 17.4% in zip code 98409 to a low of 0.5% in zip code 98388. Foster care. The percentage of Pierce County children ages 17 years and younger who received foster care placement services in 2014 (0.55%) was similar to the state's (0.58%). Almost two-thirds (62.4%) of Pierce County children under the age of 18 received some type of aid or service through the Washington State Department of Social and Health Services in 2014. This was similar to the state average of 62.1%.

Disability

Disabilities can include any one or more of five functions: hearing, vision, cognition, ambulatory, self-care and independence. Disabilities can prevent a person from living a full, normal life and limit the opportunity to hold a steady job. From 2009 to 2013, 13.3% of residents in the CHI Franciscan Health SC Hospital service area had at least one disability, compared with 10.3% of all Washington state residents.

Life expectancy and death rates provide important information about the health status of the community. Analyses of causes of death and disparities among segments of the population can help members of the community identify health needs, prioritize health concerns and develop intervention programs.

By the main category of diagnosis, 2010-2014 average Diagnosis St Clare WA

Complications of pregnancy, childbirth and the puerperium 22,960 417,235. Certain conditions originating in the perinatal period 21,059 402,625 Diseases of the circulatory system 19,659 400,913 Diseases of the digestive system 14,826 284,118 Injury and poisoning 13,779 251,011 Diseases of the musculoskeletal system and connective tissue 12,678 225,922 Diseases of the respiratory system 9,521 224,027 Infectious and parasitic diseases 7,182 154,245 Mental illness 7,168 137,040 Cancer 6,926 135,223 Diseases of the genitourinary system 6,060 130,697

Endocrine; national; and metabolic diseases and immunity disorders 5,729 89,148 Symptoms; signs; and ill-defined conditions and factors influencing health status 4,086 72,808.

Assets and Resources: CHI Franciscan Health Outpatient Nutrition Education Center. CHI Franciscan Health Diabetes Support Groups- St. Joseph Medical Center and St. Anthony Hospital. CHI Institute for Research & Innovation. CHI Franciscan Health Talks. Local parks and community centers offer public places for physical activities; some offer programs such as single-gender swim times and scholarships for children. Supplemental and Nutrition Assistance Program (SNAP-Ed). The goal of SNAP-Ed is to improve the likelihood that persons eligible for SNAP will make healthy choices within a limited budget and choose active lifestyles consistent with the current Dietary Guidelines for Americans and MyPlate. Farmers markets. The Women Infant and Children Supplemental

Nutrition Program helps pregnant women, new mothers, and young children eat well, learn about nutrition, and stay healthy.

Food banks and other feeding programs sponsored by faith-based organizations are working to provide healthier options to their customers. Ready Set Go! 5210 is a community-based initiative in Pierce County to promote healthy lifestyle choices for children, youth and families. YMCA Programs: Diabetes Prevention Program; Silver Sneakers; ACT Program Opportunities include Providing information about free or low-cost cooking and exercise programs in languages read by immigrants and refugees.

Provide healthy ethnic cooking classes for minority communities. Improving access to places for physical activity is supported by ongoing efforts of employers, coalitions, agencies, and communities. These groups are attempting to change the local environment (e.g., by creating walking trails), build new exercise facilities, provide access to existing nearby facilities, and reduce the cost of opportunities for physical activity. Improved access is typically achieved in a particular community through a multi-component strategy that includes training or education for participants.

(http://www.countyhealthrankings.org/policies/access-places-physical-activity.)

References

Braveman P, Egerter S, Williams DR. The social determinants of health: coming of age. Annu Rev Public Health. 2011; 32:381-98.   doi: 10.1146/annurev-publhealth-031210-101218. PMID: 21091195.

County Health Ranking and Roadmap (N.D). County health ranking and roadmap. Retrieved June 3, 2017 from: http://www.countyhealthrankings.org/policies/access-places-physical-activity.

CHI Franciscan Health SC Hospital Community Health Needs   Assessment   (2016).   Retrieved   from: https://www.vmfh.org/content/dam/vmfhorg/pdf/legacy-chi/website-files/about-us/community-health-needs-assessment/

Lathrop, B. 2013. Nursing Leadership in Addressing the Social Determinants of Health. *Policy, Politics, & Nursing Practice 14(1) 41–47.* DOI: 10.1177/1527154413489887

Tacoma-Pierce Community Health Department [TPCHD],

(2016). Community Health Assessment. Retrieved from

https://tpchd.org/healthy-places/public-health-

data/community-health-assessment/

McKenzie, J. F., Neiger, B. L., & Thackeray, R. (2013).

Planning, Implementing, and Evaluating Health Promotion

Program (6th ed.). Toronto: Pearson.

About The Author

My first six-months leadership trial working as a nursing supervisor at the Largest Psychiatric Hospital in Washington State, America.

Knowing that English was not taught at home growing up in the countryside in the Philippines, it was very difficult being an international student and knowing that English is my third language. I struggled with my writing. However, I was ambitious to continue my education and earn a master's degree in nursing so I could be more efficient as a nurse and serve my patients, my colleagues, and the community. Despite the difficulty in writing English, I managed to pursue and earn my master's degree in nursing at the University of Washington.

Working as a Psychiatric Nurse for over 10 years straight.

A widow, a mother, a daughter and above all, a registered nurse in the state of Washington.

I am specifically inspired by my late husband because he believed in me, and he guided me and loved me throughout our life together for over 16 years. He passed away in 2021. I am also especially thankful to my friend, who encouraged me to publish my book, Dr. Gilda Warden – she passed away in May 2024.

www.ingramcontent.com/pod-product-compliance
Lightning Source LLC
Chambersburg PA
CBHW070917120626
46546CB00001B/298